olive

100 of the very best
QUICK HEALTHY
MEALS

olive

100 of the very best QUICK HEALTHY MEALS

olive *magazine*

Copyright © Immediate Media Company London Limited 2016

The right of Immediate Media Company to be identified as the author
of this work has been asserted in accordance with the
Copyright, Designs and Patents Act 1988.

This edition firs̶t̶ ̶p̶u̶b̶l̶i̶s̶h̶e̶d̶ ̶i̶n̶ ̶G̶r̶e̶a̶t̶ ̶B̶r̶i̶t̶a̶i̶n̶ ̶2̶0̶1̶6̶
Orion, an impr̶i̶n̶t̶ ̶o̶f̶ ̶t̶h̶e̶ ̶O̶r̶i̶o̶n̶ ̶P̶u̶b̶l̶i̶s̶h̶i̶n̶g̶ ̶G̶r̶o̶u̶p̶ ̶L̶t̶d̶
Carmelite Hou̶s̶e̶
50 Victoria Em̶b̶a̶n̶k̶m̶e̶n̶t̶
London, EC4Y ̶
An Hachette U̶K̶ ̶C̶o̶m̶p̶a̶n̶y̶

10 9 8 7 6 5 4 3̶ ̶2̶ ̶1̶

All rights reserv̶e̶d̶.̶ ... under UK copyright law, this ̶p̶ublication may
only be reprod̶u̶c̶e̶d̶,̶ ̶s̶t̶o̶r̶e̶d̶ ̶o̶r̶ ̶t̶r̶a̶n̶s̶m̶i̶t̶t̶e̶d̶,̶ in any form, or by any means, ̶w̶i̶t̶h̶ ̶p̶rior permission
in writing of the ̶p̶u̶b̶l̶i̶s̶h̶e̶r̶ ̶o̶r̶,̶ ̶i̶n̶ ̶t̶h̶e̶ ̶c̶a̶s̶e̶ ̶o̶f̶ ̶r̶e̶p̶r̶o̶g̶r̶a̶p̶h̶i̶c̶ ̶r̶e̶p̶r̶o̶d̶u̶c̶t̶i̶o̶n̶ ̶i̶n̶ ̶a̶c̶c̶o̶r̶d̶ance with the
terms of licence̶s̶ ̶i̶s̶s̶u̶e̶d̶ ̶b̶y̶ ̶t̶h̶e̶ ̶C̶o̶p̶y̶r̶i̶g̶h̶t̶ ̶L̶i̶c̶e̶n̶s̶i̶n̶g̶ ̶A̶g̶e̶n̶c̶y̶.̶

A CIP catalogue̶ ̶r̶e̶c̶o̶r̶d̶ ̶f̶o̶r̶ ̶t̶h̶i̶s̶ ̶b̶o̶o̶k̶ ̶i̶s̶ ̶a̶v̶a̶i̶l̶a̶b̶l̶e̶
from the British̶ ̶L̶i̶b̶r̶a̶r̶y̶.̶

ISBN: 978 1 4091 6228 5

Designed by Goldust Design

Printed in China

The Orion Publishing Group's policy is to use papers that are natural, renewable and recyclable
and made from wood grown in sustainable forests. The logging and manufacturing processes
are expected to conform to the environmental regulations of the country of origin.

Every effort has been made to fulfil requirements with regard to reproducing copyright material.
The author and publisher will be glad to rectify any omissions at the earliest opportunity.

www.orionbooks.co.uk

For more recipes visit olivemagazine.com

Contents

Introduction

olive is Britain's brightest food magazine. More than just a collection of recipes, it's about sharing the good stuff; cooking for family and friends, discovering great restaurants and enjoying weekends away. Upmarket and glossy, our recipe photography is the best in the market. In print and online at olivemagazine.com, we keep our audience up-to-date with new food trends and provide imaginative recipes for weeknights and weekends.

When we want a quick meal, all too often we go straight for a takeaway. In *100 of the Very Best Quick Healthy Meals*, we have put together a collection of our best recipes that can be on the table in under 30 minutes – and they are all under 500 calories! Every recipe includes our trademark photography, so you know exactly what you are aiming for. From 10-minute steak tacos, easy prawn and chorizo paella to guilt-free spiced grilled paneer, this is the only collection of quick and easy healthy recipes you will need.

At **olive**, we believe you can eat well at home even if you don't have bags of time. All of the recipes in this book are ready in under 30 minutes, not including marinating or chilling time, and most can be made using easily accessible ingredients and equipment found in your kitchen. We think weekends are for more adventurous cooking so we have also included some recipes that take a little extra effort, but will be oh so worth it.

Notes and conversion tables

There are three categories of recipes throughout the *olive* books.

Easy: Most of our recipes come under this category and are very simple to put together with easy-to-find ingredients.

A little effort: These recipes require either more time, shopping for harder-to-find ingredients or a little more complicated cooking techniques.

Tricky but worth it: We have kept this book full of easy recipes so you won't find any in this category, but if you're up for a challenge, try the recipes from one of the other books in the series.

- Recipe timings are based on the total amount of time needed to finish the recipe so includes both prep and cook time.
- Provenance matters to us. Where possible, we use free-range eggs and chickens, humanely reared meat, organic dairy products, sustainably caught fish, unrefined sugar and fairly traded ingredients.
- Nutritional information is provided for all recipes. Because *olive* recipes don't always give exact quantities for ingredients such as oil and butter, nutritional quantities may not always be 100 per cent accurate. Analysis includes only the listed ingredients, not optional ingredients, such as salt, or any serving suggestions.
- Care should be taken when buying meat that you intend to eat raw or rare.
- Our recipes use large eggs, unless otherwise stated. Pregnant women, the elderly, babies and toddlers, and people who are unwell should avoid eating raw and partially cooked eggs.
- Vegetarians should always check the labels on shop-bought ingredients such as yoghurt, cheese, pesto and curry sauces, to ensure they are suitable for vegetarian consumption.
- Unless otherwise specified, if oil is listed as an ingredient, any flavourless oil such as groundnut, vegetable or sunflower oil can be used.

Liquid measurements

Metric	Imperial	Australian	US
25ml	1fl oz		
60ml	2fl oz	¼ cup	¼ cup
75ml	3fl oz		
100ml	3½fl oz		
120ml	4fl oz	½ cup	½ cup
150ml	5fl oz		
180ml	6fl oz	¾ cup	¾ cup
200ml	7fl oz		
250ml	9fl oz	1 cup	1 cup
300ml	10½fl oz	1¼ cups	1¼ cups
350ml	12½fl oz	1½ cups	1½ cups
400ml	14fl oz	1¾ cups	1¾ cups
450ml	16fl oz	2 cups	2 cups
600ml	1 pint	2½ cups	2½ cups
750ml	1¼ pints	3 cups	3 cups
900ml	1½ pints	3½ cups	3½ cups
1 litre	1¾ pints	1 quart or 4 cups	1 quart or 4 cups
1.2 litres	2 pints		
1.4 litres	2½ pints		
1.5 litres	2¾ pints		
1.7 litres	3 pints		
2 litres	3½ pints		

Oven temperature guide

	Electricity			Gas
	°C	°F	(fan) °C	Mark
Very cool	110	225	90	¼
	120	250	100	½
Cool	140	275	120	1
	150	300	130	2
Moderate	160	325	140	3
	170	350	160	4½
Moderately hot	190	375	170	5
	200	400	180	6
Hot	220	425	200	7
	230	450	210	8
Very hot	240	475	220	9

Soups and salads

Iced green gazpacho with summer salsa

20 minutes, plus chilling | serves 6–8 | easy

1 green or yellow tomato,
  quartered
½ large cucumber,
  deseeded and quartered
1 small onion, quartered
1 jalapeño chilli, deseeded
  and roughly chopped (or
  sliced from a jar)
1 green pepper, deseeded
  and quartered
2 celery sticks, roughly
  chopped
2 slices of sourdough
  bread, torn into pieces
1 garlic clove, peeled
small bunch of coriander
2 tbsp sherry vinegar
3 tbsp extra-virgin olive oil
500ml cold vegetable stock
1 yellow pepper, deseeded,
  ½ quartered and ½ diced
100g bag of watercress
  (save a handful of leaves
  to garnish)
10 radishes, sliced, to serve
2 tsp salt

Gazpacho doesn't always have to be red. We've shaken things up with this recipe for iced green gazpacho by using green and yellow tomatoes. The salsa gives it a nice touch of extra colour and crunch, too. You can speed things up by halving the vegetable stock and using 250g of ice cubes instead.

Put all the ingredients except the diced pepper, extra watercress and radishes in a bowl and add the salt. Mix, then blend in batches in a blender or food processor (a blender works best). Chill for at least 4 hours or overnight.

Pour into glasses or bowls and garnish with the radishes, diced peppers and watercress leaves.

Per serving 114 kcals, **protein** 3.5g, **carbohydrate** 12.7g, **fat** 4.9g, **saturated fat** 0.7g, **fibre** 2.7g, **salt** 0.4g

Spring greens, lemon and tortellini broth

20 minutes | serves 2 | easy

1 tbsp olive oil

1 bunch of spring onions, chopped, including the green bits

1 garlic clove, crushed

600ml vegetable stock

1 pack of veggie tortellini (about 250g)

100g baby leaf greens, stalks removed and shredded

juice of ½ lemon

grated Parmesan cheese, to serve (optional)

salt and freshly ground black pepper

This spring greens, lemon and tortellini broth looks beautiful and is delicious at any time of year. It is also low-cal and low-fat, so is perfect if you are on any type of diet.

Heat the oil in a saucepan, add the spring onions and garlic and fry gently for 5 minutes. Add the stock and cook for 5 minutes.

Add the tortellini, then after a couple of minutes, add the baby leaf greens. When the tortellini is ready, stir in the lemon juice and season. Serve with grated Parmesan if you like.

Per serving 304 kcals, **protein** 11.4g, **carbohydrate** 35.2g, **fat** 11.2g, **saturated fat** 3.3g, **fibre** 8g, **salt** 1.4g

Carrot soup with wild garlic pesto

30 minutes | serves 4 | easy

olive oil

1 onion, finely chopped

600g carrots, chopped

100g red lentils

1 litre vegetable stock

salt and freshly ground
black pepper

For the pesto

1 bunch of wild garlic
leaves

60g pine nuts

60g grana padano (or
vegetarian alternative),
plus extra, to garnish

olive oil

4 slices sourdough bread,
toasted

salt and freshly ground
black pepper

Wild garlic grows – as the name suggests – wild, so you can forage for it, but you can also buy it in markets and from some greengrocers. If you can't get hold of wild garlic you can substitute a crushed garlic clove and a large bunch of chives for it. If you can find it wild, cut it carefully from the bases of the stems rather than pulling up the bulbs.

Heat a good glug of oil in a large frying pan and fry the onion until softened, then add the carrots, stir, then fry slowly until the carrots start to brown at the edges. Tip everything into a saucepan, add the lentils and stock, and simmer for 20 minutes. Season well.

Meanwhile, make the pesto by blitzing the wild garlic, pine nuts and grana padano in the bowl of a food processor or a blender, adding enough olive oil to give it a drizzling consistency.

Blend the soup until smooth, then ladle into warmed bowls and stir in the pesto. Season and serve with slices of sourdough bread for dipping.

Per serving 449 kcals, **protein** 17.9g, **carbohydrate** 42.9g, **fat** 20.9g, **saturated fat** 4.5g, **fibre** 9.2g, **salt** 1.3g

White bean and spring green one-pot

30 minutes | serves 4 | easy

1 tsp olive oil
1 onion, chopped
1 garlic clove, crushed,
  plus ½ clove, to serve
400g can of chopped
  tomatoes
200ml vegetable stock
400g can of cannellini
  beans, drained and
  rinsed
1 tbsp chopped rosemary
  leaves, plus a pinch extra,
  to serve
150g spring greens,
  shredded
4 slices of sourdough
  bread, toasted
salt and freshly ground
  black pepper

One-pot dishes aren't just for the colder autumn and winter months. This recipe for white beans and spring greens is light and packed full of fresh, spring flavours.

Heat the oil in a saucepan. Add the onion and fry for 3 minutes until soft, then add the crushed garlic and fry for another 30 seconds. Tip in the chopped tomatoes and stock. Bring to a simmer and cook for 20 minutes until thick.

Add the cannellini beans and rosemary, and season. Cook for 5 minutes, then add the spring greens and cook until tender, adding a splash more stock if it needs it. Rub the sourdough toasts with the garlic clove half, sprinkle with a little more chopped rosemary and serve with the stew.

Per serving 294 kcals, **protein** 13.2g, **carbohydrate** 51.2g, **fat** 2.9g, **saturated fat** 0.5g, **fibre** 5.3g, **salt** 1.4g

Broccoli soup with Stilton toasts

30 minutes | serves 4 | easy

1 tbsp olive oil
1 onion, diced
1 medium potato, diced
2 celery sticks, diced
1 broccoli head, cut into
  florets, stems finely diced
750ml vegetable stock
50g Stilton
8 small slices of sourdough
  bread, toasted
snipped chives, to serve
2 tbsp toasted cashews,
  chopped, to serve
salt and freshly ground
  black pepper

This vibrant broccoli soup with Stilton toasts is the perfect antidote to the winter blues. Warming and comforting but still healthy, it is perfect for the colder months. Try a lighter cheese such as feta or goat's if you or anyone in your family doesn't like Stilton.

Heat the oil in a large saucepan, add the onion, potato and celery and fry for 10 minutes until soft. Add the broccoli and cook for a further 5 minutes before adding the stock. Simmer for 20 minutes, or until the potato is tender, and season well. Then, using a stick blender, whizz the soup until smooth and thick.

Spread the stilton over the toasts, pour the soup into warmed bowls, and top with the toasts, chives and cashews.

Per serving 377 kcals, **protein** 16.6g, **carbohydrate** 52.6g, **fat** 9.4g, **saturated fat** 3.6g, **fibre** 8g, **salt** 1.7g

Prawn and mushroom miso soup

15 minutes | serves 1 | easy

2 tbsp miso soup paste
500ml boiling water
4 shiitake mushrooms, sliced
50g pak choi, leaves separated
50g cooked, peeled prawns
30g soba noodles, soaked in boiling water for 2 minutes and drained
1 tsp soy sauce
1 tbsp chopped coriander leaves (optional)
½ red chilli, sliced (optional)

This easy prawn and mushroom miso soup is super quick, so you can have a healthy but comforting meal on the table in just 15 minutes – perfect for a mid-week supper.

Mix the miso paste in a saucepan with the boiling water and bring to a simmer. Add the mushrooms and greens, and simmer for 4 minutes until softened. Add the prawns to warm through for a minute, then remove from the heat. Add the noodles, season with soy sauce, then scatter with the coriander and chilli, if using, to serve.

Per serving 255 kcals, **protein** 15.9g, **carbohydrate** 39.7g, **fat** 2.6g, **saturated fat** 0.2g, **fibre** 5g, **salt** 4.9g

Hot-and-sour fish soup

20 minutes | serves 2 | easy

2 tbsp grated root ginger

1 dried red chilli

2 spring onions, thinly
  sliced

1 lemongrass stalk, lightly
  bashed

700ml chicken or fish stock

3 tbsp soy sauce

2 tbsp rice vinegar

400g skinless white fish,
  cut into cubes

2 handfuls of baby spinach
  leaves

2 tsp fish sauce

cooked noodles (optional)

salt and freshly ground
  black pepper

This quick and easy Asian-inspired hot-and-sour fish soup is full of big flavours like ginger, chilli and lemongrass, and will keep you full for longer.

Put the ginger, chilli, spring onions, lemongrass and stock in a saucepan and bring to a simmer. Cook for 5 minutes, then add the soy sauce, vinegar and fish, and simmer for 2 minutes. Stir in the spinach and season with the fish sauce, salt and ground black pepper. Adjust the vinegar and soy sauce if needed. Don't forget to remove the lemongrass and chilli before serving. You can add noodles to make the soup more substantial if you like.

Per serving 240 kcals, **protein** 49.7g, **carbohydrate** 4.1g, **fat** 2.1g, **saturated fat** 0.6g, **fibre** 2.8g, **salt** 6.4g

Pan-fried halibut with summer vegetable broth

20 minutes | serves 2 | easy

1 tbsp olive oil
1 shallot, diced
600ml vegetable stock (or
   enough to cover the veg)
300g summer vegetables
   (a mix of sliced leeks,
   shredded Savoy cabbage,
   peas, etc.)
50g small pasta (such as
   orzo or campanelle)
2 halibut fillets or other
   sustainable white fish
   (about 100g each)
2 tsp butter
salt and freshly ground
   black pepper

A quick recipe for halibut: light and fresh pan-fried fish served in a summery vegetable broth. The small pasta shapes will also fill you up nicely.

Heat the oil in a saucepan, add the shallot and fry for 1 minute, then add the vegetable stock and bring to the boil. Add all the vegetables (except the peas) and pasta to the pan. Simmer for 5–8 minutes, until the greens have softened a little but the pasta still has bite. Add the peas during the last minute of cooking.

Season the halibut and melt the butter in a frying pan. Fry for 2 minutes on each side, until the fish is golden, and cooked through. Season and divide the broth between 2 shallow soup bowls. Add the halibut and serve.

Per serving 353 kcals, **protein** 28.3g, **carbohydrate** 22.4g, **fat** 14.9g, **saturated fat** 2.1g, **fibre** 7.8g, **salt** 1.2g

Smoked pollock and parsnip chowder

30 minutes | serves 4 | easy

300g boneless pollock fillet
300g undyed smoked
   haddock fillet
500ml semi-skimmed milk
1 tbsp olive oil
150g smoked bacon
   lardons
1 onion, diced
1 celery stick, diced
1 small fennel bulb, diced
3 bay leaves
500g parsnips, peeled and
   cut into chunks
500ml vegetable stock
150ml single cream
1 tbsp chopped parsley
   leaves
1 tbsp chopped dill
freshly ground black
   pepper

A delicious winter fish soup that's comforting and filling. For a twist, top with a poached egg.

Put the fish and milk in a frying pan. Cover, bring to the boil, take off the heat and leave for 5 minutes until the fish is just cooked. Reserve the milk and flake the fish into big chunks, discarding the skin.

Heat the oil in a large saucepan, add the lardons and fry until they start to turn golden. Add the onion, celery, fennel, bay leaves and parsnip, and cook, stirring, until the onion is soft. Pour in the stock and reserved milk, bring to a simmer and cook for about 10 minutes, until the parsnip is tender.

Take out and blend a ladleful of the chowder, then stir it back in. Stir in the flaked fish and cream, warm through, add most of the parsley and dill and season with black pepper. Serve in warmed bowls, sprinkled with the remaining herbs.

Per serving 499 kcals, **protein** 42.9g, **carbohydrate** 27.1g, **fat** 21.9g, **saturated fat** 9.5g, **fibre** 11.3g, **salt** 3.2g

Morrocan smoky squash stew

30 minutes | serves 4 | easy

1 tbsp olive oil
1 large onion, chopped
500g butternut squash,
  peeled, deseeded
  and diced
2–3 tbsp harissa
  (depending on heat)
400g can of chickpeas,
  drained and rinsed
750ml vegetable stock
flat-leaf parsley leaves,
  chopped, to serve
crusty bread, to serve
salt and freshly ground
  black pepper

Adding chickpeas to soup means you can skip the carbs and still fill up fast. This soup is perfect for warming up on cold days.

Heat the oil in a saucepan, add the onion and fry until softened. Add the squash and cook for a few minutes, then add the harissa, chickpeas and stock. Simmer for 15–20 minutes, until the squash is tender. Stir in the parsley, season and serve in warmed bowls with crusty bread.

Per serving 193 kcals, **protein** 6.9g, **carbohydrate** 25g, **fat** 5.5g, **saturated fat** 0.6g, **fibre** 8g, **salt** 0.9g

Roots and ham hock soup

30 minutes | serves 4 | easy

butter, for frying
1 small leek, washed and
  chopped
2 carrots, diced
1 parsnip, woody core
  removed and the rest
  diced
100g swede, peeled and
  diced
1 tsp thyme leaves
700ml vegetable stock
180g ham hock, shredded
  (2 x 90g packs)
crusty bread, to serve
salt and freshly ground
  black pepper

This warming winter roots and ham hock broth is perfect for keeping the chills at bay. It's a really simple, family-friendly dish to make, and you can make a little extra to have for lunch the following day.

Melt a little butter in a frying pan and fry the leek until soft, then add the diced root veg and thyme leaves and cook for 5 minutes, until soft.

Add the vegetable stock, simmer for 10 minutes, then add the shredded ham hock and simmer for a further 5 minutes. Taste and season (you should taste the soup first as the ham hock can be quite salty). Spoon into bowls and serve with crusty bread.

Per serving 145 kcals, **protein** 10.8g, **carbohydrate** 13.5g, **fat** 3.8g, **saturated fat** 1.3g, **fibre** 7.1g, **salt** 1.9

Za'atar roasted aubergine with puy lentil salad

30 minutes | serves 2 | easy

75g puy lentils
200g baby aubergines, quartered
1 tbsp za'atar (or mix 1 tsp each of sumac, dried oregano and sesame seeds)
1 tsp oil
½ red onion, finely diced
2 tbsp sultanas
2 tsp red wine vinegar
handful of flat-leaf parsley leaves
salt and freshly ground black pepper

Za'atar is a fragrant Middle Eastern spice mix, and a great store-cupboard ingredient. Used in this recipe, it results in a dish that delivers bags of flavour.

Preheat the oven to 220°C/Fan 200°C/Gas 7. Cook the puy lentils in lightly salted, boiling water for 20 minutes, or until tender, then drain and leave to cool. Meanwhile, toss the aubergine with the za'atar and oil, then season. Tip the mixture onto a baking sheet and roast for 15–20 minutes until softened and golden.

Toss the onion, sultanas and red wine vinegar together and leave to marinate while the aubergine is cooking. Toss with the drained lentils, roasted aubergine, parsley and season. Tip everything onto a platter to serve.

Per serving 183 kcals, **protein** 3.8g, **carbohydrate** 20.3g, **fat** 1.9g, **saturated fat** 0.3g, **fibre** 4.2g, **salt** 0.2g

Warm broad bean, pea, baby leek and prosciutto salad with eggs

30 minutes | serves 4 | easy

525g podded broad beans
(double-podded if you
like)
350g fresh peas
2 tbsp olive oil
10 baby leeks, 2 thinly
sliced
3 garlic cloves, thinly sliced
4 large slices of prosciutto,
torn
2 eggs
1 handful of pea shoots
½ small bunch of chives
ciabatta toasts, to serve
(optional)
salt and freshly ground
black pepper

Broad beans are in season from June until September, and this warm salad is a fantastic way to use them. It makes the perfect lunch or light supper during the summer months.

Bring a large saucepan of lightly salted water to the boil, add the broad beans and peas and cook for 1–2 minutes, until tender but slightly al dente, then drain.

Heat the oil in a frying pan, add the whole baby leeks, sliced leeks and garlic and fry over a gentle heat until softened but not browned. Add the broad beans, peas and prosciutto with plenty of seasoning and heat through.

Remove from the heat and cover to keep warm while you fry or poach the eggs to your liking. Stir the pea shoots through the veg and prosciutto and tip onto plates. Top with the eggs, and snip over the chives. Serve with toasted ciabatta, if you like.

Per serving 358 kcals, **protein** 24.8g, **carbohydrate** 24.9g, **fat** 13.6g, **saturated fat** 2.9g, **fibre** 18.5g, **salt** 0.7g

Pear, pecan and Dolcelatte salad

15 minutes | serves 2 | easy

2 red-skinned pears, cut into slim wedges
50g rocket leaves
10 pecans, toasted and snapped in half
50g Dolcelatte, roughly chopped
2 slices of walnut bread, toasted, to serve

For the dressing

1 tbsp red wine vinegar
½ tsp Dijon mustard
2 tbsp olive oil
salt and freshly ground black pepper

A simple idea for a dinner party starter or quick lunch. Seasonal pears work brilliantly with pecan nuts and creamy Dolcelatte blue cheese for this vegetarian no-cook dish.

Toss the pear wedges and rocket leaves together and divide them between 2 plates or bowls. Top with the pecans and Dolcelatte. To make the dressing, whisk the vinegar with the mustard then whisk in the olive oil and season. Dress the salad and serve the walnut bread on the side.

Per serving 474 kcals, **protein** 9.5g, **carbohydrate** 16.9g, **fat** 39.6g, **saturated fat** 8.1g, **fibre** 6.3g, **salt** 0.9g

Veggie chopped cobb salad

20 minutes | serves 2 | easy

2–3 thick slices of ciabatta
olive oil, for drizzling
1 garlic clove, halved
2 Little Gem lettuces,
  quartered lengthways
1 large ripe avocado,
  peeled, stoned and
  cubed
2 handfuls of cherry
  tomatoes, halved
handful of chives, snipped

For the dressing
2 tsp white wine vinegar
3 tbsp soured cream
80g blue cheese, crumbled
salt and freshly ground
  black pepper

Serve this twist on the classic salad as a dinner party starter or a main course mid-week lunch or dinner. Add crispy bacon and chicken if you like.

Heat the grill to high. Put the ciabatta on a baking sheet and drizzle with oil. Grill on all sides until golden, then lightly rub with the garlic. Cut into cubes to make croutons.

To make the dressing, whisk the white wine vinegar with the soured cream, season then stir in the crumbled blue cheese.

Arrange the lettuce, avocado, tomatoes and croutons on plates. Spoon over the blue cheese dressing, sprinkle with chives and serve.

Per serving 474 kcals, **protein** 16.2g, **carbohydrate** 22.3g, **fat** 35.4g, **saturated fat** 15.1g, **fibre** 5.6g, **salt** 1.4g

Watercress, spinach and green apple salad with buttermilk dressing

20 minutes | serves 4 | easy

150g spinach, leaves
  trimmed
50g watercress
2 green apples
juice of 1 lemon

For the dressing
125ml buttermilk
3 tbsp Greek yoghurt
1 garlic clove, crushed
1 tbsp white wine vinegar
1 tbsp chives, finely
  chopped
salt and freshly ground
  black pepper

The peak season for watercress starts in April. Look for bunches with glossy leaves rather than the bags, as these are easier to prepare – just twist off the stems and you'll be left with florets.

Tip the spinach and watercress into a bowl. Core and slice the apples as thinly as you can, and toss the pieces in the lemon juice. Add them to the salad.

To make the dressing, mix all the ingredients with some salt and freshly ground black pepper in a jar or container with a lid. Put the lid on, shake well and pour the dressing over the salad to dress it. Serve as a starter or a light lunch or dinner.

Per serving 100 kcals, **protein** 4.7g, **carbohydrate** 9.5g, **fat** 4.1g, **saturated fat** 2.4g, **fibre** 2.6g, **salt** 0.3g

Winter greens and grains salad

30 minutes | serves 4 | easy

150g pearl barley or spelt

1 broccoli head, cut into very small florets

200g winter greens, such as kale or chard, shredded, and stalks removed

100g frozen edamame (soya) beans

1 bunch of spring onions, shredded

1 red chilli, finely chopped (deseeded if you like)

2 tbsp flaked almonds, toasted (optional)

salt and freshly ground black pepper

For the dressing

2 tbsp olive oil

2 tbsp red wine vinegar

½ tsp hot smoked paprika

1 tsp ground cumin

This salad is packed with plenty of veggies to build up your immune system through the winter months, but it is also so light and flavoursome it can be enjoyed year round.

Cook the pearl barley or spelt for 20–25 minutes, or according to the packet instructions, in lightly salted boiling water until tender. Drain well and tip it into a bowl.

Meanwhile, blanch the broccoli in lightly salted boiling water for 3 minutes then rinse and drain well. Do the same with the greens and edamame beans for 2 minutes.

Add the blanched vegetables, spring onions and chilli to the barley or spelt. To make the dressing, whisk the olive oil with the vinegar and spices. Pour the dressing into the bowl with the vegetables and grains, season generously and toss together. If time allows, leave for 5 minutes then toss again and serve scattered with the flaked almonds (if using).

Per serving 283 kcals, **protein** 12.2g, **carbohydrate** 35.1g, **fat** 9g, **saturated fat** 1.4g, **fibre** 6.5g, **salt** 0.3g

Three-bean and feta salad with coriander and jalapeño dressing

20 minutes | serves 4 | easy

200g green beans,
  trimmed
400g can of cannellini
  beans, drained and
  rinsed
400g can of red kidney
  beans, drained and
  rinsed
1 shallot, thinly sliced
2 large roasted red peppers
  (from a jar), drained and
  sliced
100g feta, crumbled

For the dressing
small bunch of coriander,
  leaves chopped
4 tbsp pickled jalapeños
  (from a jar), finely diced
2 tbsp olive oil
juice of 1 lemon
2 tbsp white wine vinegar
salt and freshly ground
  black pepper

A quick, easy three-bean salad makes a speedy lunch or light supper and leftovers make a great packed lunch – just save the dressing in a pot until ready to serve.

Blanch the green beans in lightly salted boiling water for 3 minutes, plunge into ice-cold water, drain and pat dry with kitchen paper.

To make the dressing, whisk the coriander, jalapeños, olive oil, lemon juice and vinegar together and season well.

Mix the cannellini and red kidney beans with the green beans. Mix the beans with the shallot and red pepper in a bowl and toss with the dressing. Scatter over the feta to serve.

Per serving 276 kcals, **protein** 14.4g, **carbohydrate** 22.6g, **fat** 11.7g, **saturated fat** 4.4g, **fibre** 11g, **salt** 1.9g

Grilled aubergine sabich salad

30 minutes | serves 6 | easy

200g bulgar wheat

6 hen's eggs

12 quail's eggs

2 medium aubergines

4 tbsp olive oil

1 tsp sumac

1 red onion, finely diced

2 celery sticks, trimmed
and diced

1 Lebanese cucumber (or
half a regular cucumber),
shredded or diced

200g plum tomatoes,
deseeded and diced

small bunch of mint, leaves
chopped

small bunch of coriander,
leaves chopped

small bunch of flat-leaf
parsley, leaves chopped

grated zest and juice of
2 lemons

2 tbsp tahini

250g Greek yoghurt

2 tbsp toasted sesame
seeds

warmed flatbread or pitta,
to serve (optional)

salt and freshly ground
black pepper

Sabich is an Israeli sandwich of pitta stuffed with fried aubergine and hard-boiled eggs. Our grilled aubergine sabich salad is a twist on this with bulgar wheat and Greek yoghurt. Serve with warm pitta or flatbread, if you like.

Put the bulgar wheat in a bowl with some seasoning, pour over enough boiling water to cover, cover with cling film and set aside while you prepare the remaining ingredients.

Sit the hen's eggs in a large pan with enough cold water to cover them. Bring to the boil, then simmer and cook for 6 minutes. Scoop them out of the pan, then carefully drop in the quail's eggs and simmer for 3 minutes. Cool all the eggs in cold water and when cool enough to handle, peel away the shells. Thickly slice the hen's eggs and halve the quail's eggs.

Heat a griddle or frying pan. Slice the aubergines into 1cm slices lengthways, brush with 2 tablespoons of the oil and griddle or fry in batches, until charred and soft. When the aubergines are cooked, sprinkle with sumac and season.

Stir the onion, celery, cucumber and tomato through the bulgar wheat with the mint, coriander and most of the parsley, plus the remaining oil, half the zest and juice and some seasoning. Slice the grilled aubergines in half lengthways and mix these through the salad.

Mix the remaining lemon juice with the tahini, yoghurt and most of the sesame seeds (save a few to sprinkle on the top). Add 1 tablespoon of water to get the dressing to a spoonable consistency.

Pile the salad and eggs on a platter. Serve with the yoghurt mixture, some warmed flatbreads or pitta, and scatter with the parsley, sesame seeds and remaining lemon zest.

Per serving 470 kcals, **protein** 19.7g, **carbohydrate** 34.5g, **fat** 26.4g, **saturated fat** 7.1g, **fibre** 7.8g, **salt** 0.4g

Butterhead salad with home-made salad cream

30 minutes | serves 4 | easy

16 spring onions, trimmed
olive oil, for brushing
4 eggs
1 butterhead lettuce, leaves
   separated
200g mixed radishes,
   halved if large
4–6 cooked beetroot,
   quartered
1 punnet of salad cress
salt and freshly ground
   black pepper

For the salad cream

4 eggs
3 tbsp white wine vinegar
½ tsp English mustard
4 tbsp groundnut oil or
   light olive oil
4 tbsp double cream
3–4 tbsp water
salt and freshly ground
   black pepper

Butterhead or English round lettuce makes a lovely base for this classic British retro salad. Home-made salad cream makes it extra special.

To make the salad cream, put the eggs into a saucepan of boiling water and cook for 10 minutes. Drain and sit in ice-cold water until cooled, then peel and halve. Remove the yolks and put them in the bowl of a small food processor (you don't need the whites).

Add the vinegar and mustard to the food processor and pulse until mixed. Gradually add the oil with the motor still running until the mixture emulsifies, then add the cream and pulse until smooth. Add 3–4 tablespoons of water, depending on how thick you want it. Season, cover and chill in the fridge until needed.

Heat a griddle pan until hot. Rub or brush the spring onions with olive oil, season and griddle, turning frequently, until chargrilled and softened.

Put the eggs for the salad into a saucepan of boiling water and cook for 7 minutes. Drop the eggs into ice-cold water, then peel and halve.

Arrange the lettuce leaves on plates and add the grilled spring onions, halved eggs, radishes and beetroot. Add a spoonful of salad cream and scatter the cress over the top.

Per serving 371 kcals, **protein** 12.3g, **carbohydrate** 7.2g, **fat** 31.9g, **saturated fat** 10.6g, **fibre** 3g, **salt** 0.5g

Spiced chicken and grain salad

30 minutes, plus marinating | serves 4 | easy

1 tsp ground cumin
1 tsp ground coriander
1 tsp ground turmeric
2 cardamom pods, seeds
  removed and crushed
½ tsp ground cinnamon
100g fat-free yoghurt
4 skinless chicken breasts
salt and freshly ground
  black pepper

For the grain salad

250g pouch of cooked
  mixed grains (such as
  quinoa and wild rice)
juice of ½ lemon, plus
  wedges to serve
1 tsp garam masala
2 large tomatoes, diced
2 carrots, grated
1 small red onion, finely
  diced
handful of coriander
  leaves, plus extra to serve
handful of rocket leaves
1 tsp groundnut or olive oil
salt and freshly ground
  black pepper

The chicken for this spiced yoghurt chicken and grain salad can be prepped the night before, then you can have dinner ready in just 30 minutes.

Mix the cumin, coriander, turmeric, crushed cardamom seeds and cinnamon with the yoghurt and season well. Pour over the chicken breasts, making sure they are well coated, then cover and chill. Leave to marinate for 2 hours or overnight.

Heat the oven to 200°C/Fan 180°C/Gas 6. Transfer the marinated chicken to a baking tray and cook for 20–25 minutes, or until the breasts are cooked through, and the spice crust has turned golden.

While the chicken is cooking, mix all the grain salad ingredients together with the oil and some seasoning. Add more lemon juice if you like. Tip the salad onto a serving platter. Remove the chicken from the oven and slice the breasts. Place the slices on the grain salad. Serve with lemon wedges and more coriander scattered over the top.

Per serving 333 kcals, protein 36.9g, carbohydrate 28.4g, fat 6.8g, saturated fat 1.2g, fibre 5.3g, salt 0.7g

Thai chicken noodle salad

30 minutes | serves 2 | easy

1 skinless chicken breast

1 tbsp Thai green curry paste

60g flat rice noodles, cooked, drained and rinsed

1 spring onion, shredded

2 carrots, peeled and shredded (using a spiralizer or julienne grater)

1½ red chillies, deseeded and shredded

1 cucumber, shredded

½ small bunch of coriander, leaves picked

½ small bunch of mint, leaves picked and chopped

salt and freshly ground black pepper

For the coconut-lime dressing

grated zest and juice of 2 limes

2 tbsp half-fat coconut milk (freeze the rest of the can)

1 tsp fish sauce

½ red chilli, deseeded and finely diced

This chicken noodle salad is full of delicious, vibrant Thai flavours, is quick and easy to make, and healthy too.

Heat the grill to high. Rub the chicken with the curry paste and grill for 4 minutes on each side, or until cooked through, then set aside to rest. Make the coconut-lime dressing by mixing all the ingredients together.

Toss the cooked noodles, spring onion, carrots, chilli, cucumber and herbs together with half the dressing, and pile onto 2 plates. Slice the chicken, add it to the salad and season, then drizzle with the remaining dressing to serve.

Per serving 182 kcals, **protein** 17.7g, **carbohydrate** 17.5g, **fat** 3.8g, **saturated fat** 1.1g, **fibre** 4g, **salt** 1g

Steak and winter greens

30 minutes | serves 2 | easy

oil, for frying
1 onion, sliced
2 garlic cloves, crushed
6 kale stems, stalks stripped
   out and discarded, and
   leaves roughly chopped
6 chard stems, stalks
   stripped out and
   discarded, and leaves
   roughly chopped
6 Brussels sprouts, trimmed
   and thinly sliced
2 tbsp chicken stock
1 large or 2 small fillet
   steak(s)
1 tsp cracked black pepper
1 tsp Dijon mustard
2 anchovies, finely
   chopped
2 tsp red wine vinegar
salt

Topping this warm winter salad with steak makes it feel like a real treat – a perfect way to pep up your week. Fry the steak for a few seconds longer if you like it more well done.

Heat a little oil in a frying pan, add the onion and fry for about 8 minutes, until soft. Add the garlic and fry for 1 minute, then add the greens and stock, cover and cook for 5 minutes.

Meanwhile, rub the steak(s) with a little oil and press in the cracked black pepper. Season with salt. Heat a frying pan or griddle until very hot, then cook the steak for 2 minutes on one side and 3 minutes on the other. Remove and set aside to rest for 5 minutes.

Check the greens are tender, season, then stir in the mustard, anchovies and vinegar. Slice the steak and serve with any juices and the greens.

Per serving 405 kcals, **protein** 39.g, **carbohydrate** 28.4g, **fat** 13.6g, **saturated fat** 4g, **fibre** 6.2g, **salt** 1.8g

Green goddess salad

20 minutes | serves 2 | easy

50g quinoa

100g peas, blanched

2 tbsp lemon juice

50g bag of watercress

½ avocado, peeled, stoned
  and sliced

4 slices of smoked streaky
  bacon, grilled until crisp
  and golden

salt and freshly ground
  black pepper

For the green goddess dressing

2 spring onions, chopped
  (including the green bits)

juice of ½ lemon

2 tbsp mayonnaise

small bunch of basil, leaves
  chopped

small bunch of chives,
  snipped

2–3 tbsp water

salt and freshly ground
  black pepper

Named after the green herb dressing, this is feel-good food at its best. Add watercress for a peppery kick and crispy bacon for saltiness.

Cook the quinoa according to the packet instructions, then rinse and drain really well. Transfer it to a bowl and toss with the peas, lemon juice and some seasoning.

Whizz all the dressing ingredients, except the water and seasoning, to a purée in a small food processor or blender. Add the water to loosen it to a drizzling consistency. Season.

Arrange the quinoa, watercress and avocado on plates or in bowls. Drizzle over the dressing then crumble over the bacon.

Per serving 483 kcals, **protein** 18.3g, **carbohydrate** 20.1g, **fat** 35.3g, **saturated fat** 8.1g, **fibre** 6g, **salt** 2g

Smoked salmon and quail's egg Caesar salad

20 minutes | serves 2 | easy

9 quail's eggs

1 thick slice of sourdough
  bread, cubed

2 tsp olive oil

1 Little Gem lettuce, leaves
  separated and torn

handful of mixed leaves

150g smoked salmon, torn

1 tbsp small capers, rinsed

small bunch of chives,
  snipped

salt and freshly ground
  black pepper

For the Caesar dressing

½ garlic clove, crushed

2 anchovies

25g Parmesan cheese,
  finely grated

1 tbsp Greek yoghurt

2 tbsp olive oil

juice of ½ lemon

freshly ground black
  pepper

A slightly fancier take on your usual Caesar salad, this version is topped with salmon, quail's eggs and capers – perfect for a dinner party starter or light meal.

Preheat the oven to 200°C/Fan 180°C/Gas 6. Bring a pan of water to the boil, add the quail's eggs and boil for 3 minutes, then drain and put the eggs into ice-cold water to stop them cooking.

Toss the sourdough bread cubes with the olive oil and some seasoning on a baking tray. Put the tray in the oven and bake for 8–10 minutes, or until the cubes are golden and crisp.

To make the dressing, put the crushed garlic clove and anchovies in a mortar and crush together with a pestle. Add the Parmesan, yoghurt, olive oil and lemon juice, add a little black pepper, and mix together.

Peel and halve the quail's eggs. Place the lettuce and the mixed leaves, halved quail's eggs, sourdough croutons, smoked salmon, capers and chives on a platter. Spoon over the dressing and toss together gently.

Per serving 450 kcals, **protein** 34.5g, **carbohydrate** 15g, **fat** 27.7g, **saturated fat** 8g, **fibre** 2.3g, **salt** 4.3g

Smoked trout and cannellini bean salad

15 minutes | serves 2 | easy

½ red onion, very thinly
  sliced
1 tbsp red wine vinegar
2 tbsp olive oil
400g can of cannellini
  beans, drained and
  rinsed
125g smoked trout, flaked
50g rocket leaves
crusty bread or toast,
  to serve
salt and freshly ground
  black pepper

This recipe for smoked trout and cannnellini bean salad is ready in just 15 minutes. It's perfect for lunch or a lighter supper throughout the summer.

Put the onion in a bowl with the vinegar and olive oil. Season generously and set aside for 10 minutes.

Add the beans and trout to the bowl and toss everything together. Add the rocket, toss gently, then serve with crusty bread or toast.

Per serving 316 kcals, **protein** 22.5g, **carbohydrate** 18g, **fat** 15.2g, **saturated fat** 2.7g, **fibre** 8.4g, **salt** 1.1g

Smoked trout and asparagus Niçoise

20 minutes | serves 4 | easy

500g baby new potatoes,
  scrubbed and halved
125g asparagus tips
12 quail's eggs
4 smoked trout fillets,
  roughly broken into
  large pieces
2 handfuls of black olives,
  pitted

For the dressing
5 tbsp extra-virgin olive oil
2 tbsp white wine vinegar
1 tbsp Dijon mustard
1 garlic clove, crushed
salt and freshly ground
  black pepper

This is a twist on the classic Niçoise salad. It's also delicious with the traditional tuna too.

Boil the potatoes in lightly salted boiling water for 10 minutes, or until tender, adding the asparagus for the final 4 minutes, then drain. Boil the quail's eggs for 2 minutes, drain and then rinse under cold running water until cool enough to handle. Peel and halve the eggs.

To make the dressing, whisk the oil with the vinegar, mustard, garlic and season. Divide the eggs, asparagus, potatoes, trout and olives between 4 plates or arrange on a platter. Drizzle over the dressing and serve.

Per serving 393 kcals, **protein** 20.2g, **carbohydrate** 21.9g, **fat** 24.6g, **saturated fat** 4.4g, **fibre** 4.2g, **salt** 1.9g

Sea bass Thai noodle salad

30 minutes | serves 4 | easy

2 shallots, finely sliced
3 tbsp lime juice, plus
  2 whole limes to serve,
  halved
2 tbsp rice wine vinegar
1 tbsp fish sauce
3 tbsp golden caster sugar
1 red bird's eye chilli,
  finely sliced (deseeded
  if you like)
250g rice noodle vermicelli
4 sea bass fillets
oil, for brushing
½ cucumber, peeled, seeds
  removed and sliced
handful of mint, leaves
  finely sliced
large handful of coriander,
  leaves chopped
salt and freshly ground
  black pepper

This light, fragrant, Thai-inspired noodle salad with sea bass is a delicious lighter meal. Sea bass has a superb slightly sweet, meaty texture, which works really well in this dish.

Put the shallots, lime juice, vinegar, fish sauce and caster sugar in a bowl and mix until the sugar dissolves, then add the chilli and set aside. Meanwhile, cook the rice noodles according to the packet instructions and drain well.

Brush the skin of the sea bass fillets with oil and season the flesh side. Heat a frying pan until very hot and add the fillets skin-side down. (Use 2 pans, or do this in 2 batches.) Cook the fillets for 3 minutes, then put the pan under a hot grill to finish the tops: you want the fish just cooked, with a crisp skin.

Toss the cooked noodles in the shallot mix with the cucumber and herbs, keeping back some of the herbs for the top. Divide the noodles between 4 shallow bowls and put a fish fillet, skin-side up, on top of each with a lime half to squeeze over.

Per serving 428 kcals, **protein** 27.5g, **carbohydrate** 65.4g, **fat** 6.2g, **saturated fat** 0.8g, **fibre** 0.6g, **salt** 1.1g

Smoked mackerel and roasted beetroot salad

30 minutes | serves 4 | easy

250g cooked beetroot,
   quartered
1 tsp olive oil
100g watercress
280g pack of peppered
   smoked mackerel
salt and freshly ground
   black pepper

For the dressing

1 tbsp horseradish (freshly
   grated or creamed)
2 tbsp low-fat natural
   yoghurt
1 tsp Dijon mustard
1 tbsp chopped dill
juice of ½ lemon
salt and freshly ground
   black pepper

Mackerel and beetroot match perfectly with each other and this is a really quick and easy way to partner them. The peppery watercress and kick of horseradish adds plenty of flavour so you won't need lots of dressing.

Heat the oven to 200°C/Fan 180°C/Gas 6. Toss the beetroot quarters with the oil, season, tip them onto a baking tray and roast for 20 minutes. Remove them from the oven and leave to cool a little.

To make the dressing, mix the horseradish, yoghurt, mustard and half the dill and season. Add a little lemon juice to loosen.

Divide the watercress between 4 plates, break up the smoked mackerel and scatter it over the top with the beetroot wedges. Drizzle over the dressing and remaining dill to serve.

Per serving 310 kcals, protein 16.7g, carbohydrate 7.8g, fat 23.1g, saturated fat 4.7g, fibre 2.4g, salt 1.7g

Crab and fennel salad with mandarin dressing

20 minutes | serves 2 | easy

½ fennel bulb, very thinly
  sliced
1 celery stick, shredded
1 dessert apple, cut into
  slim wedges
100g white crabmeat
handful of watercress
sourdough bread slices,
  toasted, to serve

**For the mandarin
dressing**
grated zest and juice of
  1 mandarin
½ tsp sesame oil
2cm piece of fresh root
  ginger, peeled and finely
  grated
1 tsp white wine vinegar
1 tbsp snipped chives
salt and freshly ground
  black pepper

This crab, fennel, apple, celery and watercress salad is so easy to put together and is very light and refreshing. Serve with toasted sourdough on the side to help scoop up the crab.

To make the dressing, whisk all the ingredients, except the salt and pepper, together. Season and set aside.

Add the fennel, celery and apple to the dressing and toss together. Just before serving, gently mix in the crab and watercress. Serve with toasted sourdough.

Per serving 120 kcals, **protein** 11.3g, **carbohydrate** 7.9g, **fat** 3.9g, **saturated fat** 0.5g, **fibre** 3.8g, **salt** 0.6g

Very speedy meals

Egg white omelette with kale and sweet potato

15 minutes | serves 2 | easy

1 sweet potato, peeled and
cut into small dice
handful of kale leaves,
tough stems removed
and leaves shredded
olive oil spray
1 small onion, diced
½ red chilli, deseeded
and diced
grated zest and juice of
1 lime, plus wedges to
serve
4 egg whites
2 tbsp snipped chives or
chopped parsley leaves
salt and freshly ground
black pepper

This egg white omelette is a great skinny alternative to a normal omelette, but as it's filled with delicious, healthy ingredients, you won't feel like you're missing out and it will keep you feeling fuller for longer.

Cook the sweet potato in lightly salted boiling water for 4 minutes, until tender. Scoop it out with a slotted spoon and drain. Cook the shredded kale in the same water for 2 minutes, then drain well.

Spray a frying pan with olive oil and fry the onion for 5 minutes, until soft. Add the sweet potato and fry for 5 minutes, until the edges start to crisp up and turn golden. Add the kale, chilli and lime zest and juice, and stir for a minute. Remove from the heat and set aside.

Whisk the egg whites, 2 at a time, with some seasoning and half the chopped herbs. Spray a separate frying pan with oil, heat, then add the beaten egg whites to make a thin omelette. Cook until set, then add half the filling mix and fold. Repeat with the remaining 2 egg whites, the rest of the filling and the herbs. Serve with lime wedges.

Per serving 169 kcals, **protein** 8.5g, **carbohydrate** 26.7g, **fat** 1.8g, **saturated fat** 0.4g, **fibre** 6g, **salt** 0.5g

Avocado and smoked salmon toasts

15 minutes | serves 2 | easy

1 avocado
2 tbsp fat-free yoghurt
juice of ½ lemon
2 slices of rye bread,
  toasted
pinch of cayenne pepper
75g smoked salmon
¼ cucumber, ribboned with
  a vegetable peeler
handful of salad cress
salt and freshly ground
  black pepper

For the dressing
½ red chilli, deseeded and
  finely diced
1 tbsp finely chopped mint
  leaves
grated zest and juice of
  ½ lemon
1 tomato, finely diced
1 tsp white wine vinegar
salt and freshly ground
  black pepper

Creamy avocado and delicious smoked salmon feel like an indulgence, but this dish comes in at under 300 calories meaning you can have a little bit of luxury any day of the week or any time of day.

Make the dressing by mixing all the ingredients together with some seasoning.

Halve the avocado, remove the stone and scoop the flesh into a bowl. Add the yoghurt and lemon juice and mash everything with a fork. Season well with salt and black pepper.

Divide the avocado between the pieces of toasted rye bread, sprinkle over a little cayenne pepper and add the smoked salmon and cucumber. Spoon over the dressing, then top with the salad cress.

Per serving 296 kcals, **protein** 16.1g, **carbohydrate** 17.7g, **fat** 16.6g, **saturated fat** 3.4g, **fibre** 5.8g, **salt** 2.3g

Sourdough with spinach, egg and mustard

15 minutes | serves 2 | easy

knob of butter, plus extra
for spreading
1 small shallot, finely
chopped
200g young spinach leaves,
washed if needed
2 tsp wholegrain mustard
1 tsp sherry vinegar
4 slices of sourdough
bread
2–4 eggs, fried
salt and freshly ground
black pepper

The best all-day breakfast recipe: fried eggs on sourdough toast. Add spinach and a punchy mustard-shallot dressing and you've got your weekend off to a great start.

Melt the butter in a frying pan and add the shallot. Cook until softened, then add the spinach with a tiny splash of water and heat until just wilted. Stir in the mustard and sherry vinegar and season.

Toast the sourdough and spread with a little more butter. Pile the spinach on top and finish with the fried eggs.

Per serving 372 kcals, protein 15.7g, carbohydrate 26.5g, fat 21.7g, saturated fat 9.7g, fibre 4.2g, salt 1.7g

Super store-cupboard salad

15 minutes | serves 4 | easy

100g frozen edamame
  (soya beans)
100g frozen peas
400g can of chickpeas,
  drained and rinsed
250g pouch of cooked
  spelt
¼ red onion, very finely
  chopped
juice of 1 lemon
2 tbsp olive oil
1 tsp cumin seeds
small bunch of mint, leaves
  chopped
salt and freshly ground
  pepper

This super store-cupboard salad is perfect for a speedy mid-week supper. It's ready in just 15 minutes, under 300 calories and vegetarian. It serves four, but you can always serve fewer people and have leftovers for lunch.

Drop the beans and peas into a saucepan of lightly salted, boiling water and cook for 2 minutes, then drain and cool under cold running water.

Tip them into a bowl and add the chickpeas, spelt and onion. Whisk the lemon juice with the olive oil and the cumin seeds. Add the mixture to the bowl with the peas, beans, chickpeas and spelt, season well and toss everything together. Add the mint, toss and serve.

Per serving 296 kcals, **protein** 12.3g, **carbohydrate** 32.9g, **fat** 10.8g, **saturated fat** 1.4g, **fibre** 8.8g, **salt** 0.6g

Courgetti with pesto and balsamic tomatoes

15 minutes | serves 1 | easy

8 baby plum tomatoes,
   4 halved and 4 left whole
1 tsp olive oil
½ garlic clove, crushed
1 tbsp balsamic vinegar
1 large courgette, cut into
   spaghetti with a spiralizer
   or very thinly shredded
   into noodles
2 tbsp fresh vegetarian
   pesto
1 tbsp pine nuts, toasted
salt and freshly ground
   black pepper

Who needs pasta when you can have spiralized courgette? Try our easy 'courgetti' recipe, made with baby plum tomatoes, garlic, pesto, pine nuts and a lot of courgette noodles.

Toss the tomatoes (halved and whole) with the oil, garlic and balsamic vinegar and some seasoning. Tip them into a frying pan and cook for 5 minutes, until the whole tomatoes start to burst and are coated in the balsamic vinegar.

Place the courgette 'spaghetti' in a heatproof bowl, pour a kettle of just-boiled water over the courgette and leave for 30 seconds. Drain well, toss with the pesto and season generously. Add the tomatoes and toasted pine nuts to serve.

Per serving 459 kcals, **protein** 12.6g, **carbohydrate** 28.7g, **fat** 29.8g, **saturated fat** 4g, **fibre** 13.3g, **salt** 1.1g

Halloumi with caper, lemon and chilli dressing

10 minutes | serves 3 | easy

250g pouch of mixed
   cooked grains (such as
   spelt or quinoa)
1 lemon, halved
handful of mint, coriander
   or parsley leaves
   (or a mixture), chopped
1 large tomato, diced
2 spring onions, chopped
1 block of halloumi
   (about 250g), sliced
salt and freshly ground
   black pepper

For the dressing
1 tbsp olive oil
juice of ½ lemon
2 tsp small capers, rinsed
1 red chilli, finely chopped
   (deseeded if you like)
¼ small garlic clove,
   crushed

This halloumi salad is super filling thanks to the mixed grains. Serve as a quick starter or main meal.

Tip the grains into a bowl. Add a good squeeze of lemon juice and some seasoning, then toss through the herbs, tomato and spring onions. Heat a non-stick frying pan and fry the halloumi until golden.

To make the dressing, whisk the olive oil with the lemon juice, capers, chilli and garlic. Put the grain salad on 3 plates. Top with the halloumi slices and spoon over the dressing.

Per serving 482 kcals, **protein** 24.4g, **carbohydrate** 28.3g, **fat** 29.2g, **saturated fat** 14.6g, **fibre** 4.1g, **salt** 2.5g

Broccoli, chilli and lemon wholewheat pasta

15 minutes | serves 2 | easy

150g wholewheat spaghetti
300g tenderstem broccoli,
  roughly chopped
1 tsp oil
1 shallot, sliced
large pinch of dried red
  chilli flakes, plus extra
  to serve
1 garlic clove, crushed
grated zest and juice of
  1 lemon
salt and freshly ground
  black pepper

Using wholewheat pasta adds fibre without affecting the taste of this finished dish. Broccoli, chilli and lemon make the easiest home-made pasta sauce for a quick dinner.

Cook the spaghetti according to the packet instructions, adding the broccoli to the pan for the last 3 minutes, then drain.

Meanwhile, heat the oil in a large frying pan, and gently fry the shallot, chilli flakes and garlic. Add the drained pasta and broccoli to the pan, and mix in the lemon zest and juice. Season well. Divide the dish between pasta bowls and serve.

Per serving 311 kcals, **protein** 14.6g, **carbohydrate** 46.8g, **fat** 4.6g, **saturated fat** 0.6g, **fibre** 11.7g, **salt** 0.2g

15-minute Szechuan pork

15 minutes | serves 4 | easy

1 tbsp groundnut oil
1 garlic clove, crushed
1 red chilli, diced
  (deseeded if you like)
1 tbsp grated fresh root
  ginger
1 tsp Szechuan
  peppercorns, crushed
1 pork fillet (about 400g),
  trimmed and cut into
  strips
bunch of spring onions,
  trimmed and sliced
150g green beans,
  trimmed and blanched
  for 2 minutes
2 tbsp soy sauce
4 egg noodle nests, cooked
salt and freshly ground
  black pepper

As the name suggests, this Szechuan pork recipe is super speedy, making it a perfect meal when you're short of time. You can easily replace the pork with chicken or tofu, if you prefer.

Heat the oil in a wok, and fry the garlic, chilli, ginger and Szechuan pepper for 2 minutes, until fragrant. Add the pork strips and fry for 8–10 minutes until cooked through.

Meanwhile, cook the egg noodles according to the packet instructions. Add most of the spring onions to the pork, and fry for a further minute. Add the blanched green beans, and stir through the soy sauce. Stir in the cooked noodles, season and divide the dish between 4 bowls. Top with the remaining spring onion to serve.

Per serving 470 kcals, **protein** 34.5g, **carbohydrate** 65.2g, **fat** 7.1g, **saturated fat** 1.4g, **fibre** 3.9g, **salt** 2.8g

Pork saltimbocca

15 minutes | serves 1 | easy

50g orzo, to serve

100g piece of pork tenderloin cut into 1cm-thick slices

2–3 pieces of Parma ham

4–6 sage leaves

olive oil, for frying

knob of butter

3 tbsp marsala wine

salt and freshly ground black pepper

Saltimbocca is Italian for 'jumps in the mouth'. This dish is usually made with veal, but you can also make it using chicken or pork, as we have here. The slices of ham help to keep the pork from drying out. Bump up the ingredients to serve as a family or dinner party meal.

Cook the orzo according to packet instructions. Meanwhile, put the slices of pork between 2 pieces of baking paper and bash them thinner with a rolling pin or the base of a pan. Pull the Parma ham into pieces big enough to fit over the pork, and lay over each piece of pork, then put a sage leaf on top. Pin them together with a cocktail stick.

Heat some oil with the butter in a frying pan, add the pork pieces, sage-side down, and cook for 2 minutes, then turn them over and cook for another minute. Season. Add the marsala and bubble the alcohol off for a few minutes. Serve with the orzo and use the remaining sauce to dress the pasta.

Per serving 334 kcals, **protein** 30.6g, **carbohydrate** 6.5g, **fat** 15.3g, **saturated fat** 5.8g, **fibre** 0g, **salt** 2.1g

10-minute steak tacos

10 minutes | serves 2 | easy

1 large or 2 small sirloin or
  rump steaks (about
  250g), fat trimmed
oil, to coat
½ tsp ground cumin
¼ tsp smoked paprika
2 tbsp chopped pickled
  jalepeños (from a jar)
6 tbsp soured cream
½ bunch of coriander,
  leaves chopped, plus
  extra to serve
4 corn tortillas, warmed,
  to serve
salt and freshly ground
  black pepper
6 radishes, sliced, to serve
4 spring onions, sliced,
  to serve
100g feta, crumbled,
  to serve

**Steak always feels like a treat, but with these 10-minute steak tacos
you can have it mid-week too. Lightly spiced with paprika and cumin,
and with crunchy radishes and salty feta, these tacos are sure to be
a new favourite.**

Rub the steaks with oil, then rub in the spices, season and set aside.
Mix the jalepeños, soured cream and coriander in a bowl and season.

Heat a non-stick frying pan until hot then sear the steak for 2 minutes on
each side. Rest for a couple of minutes, then slice and serve with warm
tortillas and the radish, spring onion and feta.

Per serving 450 kcals, **protein** 36.9g, **carbohydrate** 4.2g, **fat** 31.5g, **saturated fat** 17.8g, **fibre** 0.9g, **salt** 2.2g

Chargrilled chilli prawns with cucumber salad

15 minutes | serves 2 | easy

1 garlic clove, crushed
1 red chilli, deseeded and
   diced
grated zest and juice of
   1 lime
small bunch of flat-leaf
   parsley, leaves chopped
2 tbsp olive oil, plus 1 tsp
   for the cucumber salad
200g raw, unpeeled prawns
½ cucumber, cut into
   ribbons
2 spring onions, sliced
1 tbsp rice vinegar
crusty bread, toasted,
   to serve
salt and freshly ground
   black pepper

This dish may look tricky, but it is very quick and easy to make, and is guaranteed to make you feel like you are on holiday. Serve with a small bowl of water with a slice of lemon to clean your hands after peeling the prawns.

Mix the garlic, chilli, lime zest and half the parsley with the olive oil and season, then toss with the prawns. Mix the cucumber with the spring onions, remaining parsley, rice vinegar and the teaspoon of olive oil and season.

Grill or barbecue the prawns for 2 minutes on each side, until cooked through. Drizzle over the lime juice and serve with the cucumber salad and crusty bread.

Per serving 206 kcals, **protein** 18.9g, **carbohydrate** 2.4g, **fat** 13.4g, **saturated fat** 1.9g, **fibre** 1.5g, **salt** 0.5g

Thai smoked trout salad

15 minutes | serves 1 | easy

1 red chilli, deseeded and
  diced
1 shallot, sliced
juice of 1 lime
2 tsp fish sauce
50g bean sprouts,
  blanched
½ cucumber, sliced
handful of coriander leaves
handful of mint leaves
handful of Thai basil leaves
30g rice noodles, cooked,
  drained and rinsed
50g hot smoked trout fillet,
  flaked
salt and freshly ground
  black pepper

The kind of salad we love: fresh, clean Thai flavours, smoked fish and noodles with a hit of chilli and lime.

Whisk the chilli, shallot, lime juice and fish sauce together. Add the bean sprouts, cucumber, herbs, rice noodles and smoked trout, season and toss with the dressing. Scatter with a few more herbs to serve, if you like.

Per serving 215 kcals, **protein** 16g, **carbohydrate** 30.3g, **fat** 3.3g, **saturated fat** 0.8g, **fibre** 2.2g, **salt** 3g

Griddled tuna with pineapple salsa

15 minutes | serves 2 | easy

2 tuna steaks
1 tsp oil
cooked new potatoes,
 to serve
salt and freshly ground
 black pepper

For the salsa
120g pineapple, finely
 diced
1 shallot, finely diced
1 tomato, seeded and
 diced
1 red chilli, deseeded and
 diced
juice of ½ lime
2 tbsp chopped coriander
 leaves
salt and freshly ground
 black pepper

Tuna is very easy to prepare, so it makes a great meal when you're short of time. The sweetness from the pineapple is off-set by the spice from the chilli, which gives this dish a distinct Caribbean feel.

Brush the steaks with the oil and season generously.

To make the salsa, toss the pineapple, shallot, tomato, chilli and lime juice together in a bowl and season well. Heat a griddle pan to very hot, and cook the tuna steaks for 1 minute on each side, or longer if you like. Stir the coriander through the salsa and serve with the tuna and new potatoes.

Per serving 242 kcals, **protein** 33.9g, **carbohydrate** 7.3g, **fat** 8.2g, **saturated fat** 1.9g, **fibre** 1.6g, **salt** 0.2g

Meat-free meals

Leek, mushroom and spinach soufflé omelette

25 minutes | serves 1 | easy

2 handfuls of spinach
  leaves
olive oil, for frying
knob of butter, plus extra
  for frying
1 small leek, washed,
  trimmed and sliced
handful of chestnut
  mushrooms, roughly
  chopped
2 eggs, separated
1 tbsp finely grated
  Parmesan cheese
salt and freshly ground
  black pepper

This 'soufflé' omelette is lighter and fluffier than your normal version. Filled with spinach, leeks, mushrooms and melted cheese, this is a very impressive omelette indeed.

Put the spinach in a sieve and pour over a kettle-full of boiling water. Cool and squeeze out the excess moisture.

Heat a little oil in a non-stick frying pan with the butter, add the leek and mushrooms, season then cook until soft. Remove and set to one side.

Whisk the egg yolks with 1 tablespoon of water in a bowl and season. Whisk the whites in a separate bowl until they form soft peaks then fold them gently into the egg yolks, retaining as much air as possible.

Add more butter to the pan, then add the eggs. Cook for 1 minute or until the base is set, then put the mushroom and leek mix, the spinach and grated cheese on one half of the omelette. Flip the bare half over the filling. Cook for a few minutes more, then serve.

Per serving 279 kcals, **protein** 19g, **carbohydrate** 3.1g, **fat** 21.1g, **saturated fat** 8.1g, **fibre** 2.9g, **salt** 0.7g

Broccoli and roasted red pepper frittata

20 minutes | serves 4 | easy

1 tsp oil

large pinch of red chilli
flakes, plus extra to serve
(optional)

4 roasted red peppers
(from a jar), drained and
sliced

300g tenderstem broccoli,
halved, blanched for
3 minutes and drained

8 eggs, beaten

4 tbsp whole milk

handful of basil leaves

salad, to serve

salt and freshly ground
black pepper

This frittata makes for a quick and healthy supper. Try swapping in different ingredients too – it is great for using up soon-to-be expired veggies.

Heat the oil in an ovenproof frying pan and add the chilli flakes, peppers and broccoli for a few minutes. Whisk the eggs and milk together and season well.

Add the egg mix to the pan, pulling in the sides with a wooden spoon until the edges start to set. Scatter over the basil, and put the pan under a hot grill for 5 minutes until puffed, golden brown and the egg has set. Serve with a salad and some more chilli flakes, if you like.

Per serving 223 kcals, **protein** 17.8g, **carbohydrate** 5.5g, **fat** 13.9g, **saturated fat** 3.6g, **fibre** 2.6g, **salt** 0.4g

Spinach and feta chickpea pancakes

30 minutes | serves 2 | easy

200g chickpea flour
  (gram flour)
2 tbsp snipped chives,
  plus extra to serve
300ml cold water
1 tsp olive oil, plus extra
  for brushing
1 onion, diced
1 garlic clove, crushed
freshly grated nutmeg,
  to taste
300g baby spinach leaves,
  chopped, blanched and
  drained well, plus handful
  of raw leaves
50g low-fat feta, crumbled,
  plus extra to serve
salt and freshly ground
  black pepper

These spinach and feta chickpea pancakes make for a delicious quick and healthy meal, at any time of the day. Chickpea flour (gram flour) is gluten-free and contains more protein than other flours.

Whisk the flour, chives and lots of seasoning with the water. Leave to sit for at least 15 minutes.

Heat the oil in a frying pan and gently cook the onion for 8 minutes, until soft but not browned. Add the garlic, cook for a further minute, then add a grating of nutmeg and the spinach, and stir. Scatter in the feta and season with black pepper.

Brush a non-stick frying pan with olive oil, then spoon enough batter into the pan (swirling it) to make a thin pancake. Turn it over after 2 minutes, or when the edges have set. Cook for 2 minutes more then add a spoonful of the spinach mix onto half of the pancake and fold the other half over the filling. Repeat until all the batter and filling have been used – you should make about 4 pancakes. As soon as they're made, keep them warm in a low oven while you make the rest. Serve with fresh spinach leaves and some snipped chives.

Per serving 421 kcals, **protein** 16.7g, **carbohydrate** 64.8g, **fat** 7.5g, **saturated fat** 0.9g, **fibre** 14g, **salt** 0.6g

Kale and sweet potato hash

20 minutes | serves 2 | easy

200g kale, washed

1 large sweet potato,
   peeled and cut into small
   chunks

oil, for frying

1 garlic clove, finely sliced

4 spring onions, sliced

1 red chilli, sliced
   (deseeded if you like)

2 eggs

hot chilli sauce, to serve
   (optional)

salt and freshly ground
   black pepper

Healthy and comforting, this kale and sweet potato hash with a chilli kick is fresh, light and filling. It also makes a great brunch dish for the weekend.

Drop the kale into a saucepan of boiling, salted water for 3 minutes, then scoop it out with a slotted spoon and rinse under cold running water. Drain and roughly chop. Cook the sweet potato in the same pan for 5–6 minutes until just tender, then drain well.

Heat a little oil in a frying pan. Add the sweet potato, and cook until it crisps up a bit. Add the garlic, spring onions and chilli, cook for a couple of minutes, then add the blanched kale and cook for a few minutes more, letting it take on all the other flavours. Season. Meanwhile, fry the eggs.

Spoon the hash onto 2 plates and top each with a fried egg. Serve with hot chilli sauce, if you like.

Per serving 304 kcals, **protein** 14.3g, **carbohydrate** 31.2g, **fat** 12.7g, **saturated fat** 3g, **fibre** 3.9g, **salt** 0.4g

Creamy courgette and polenta tart

30 minutes | serves 4 | easy

800ml vegetable stock
200g instant polenta
olive oil, for frying
3-4 courgettes, sliced
2 garlic cloves, crushed
100g mascarpone
2 tbsp grated Parmesan
  cheese
large handful of rocket,
  to serve
salt and freshly ground
  black pepper

Instant polenta makes a perfect base for a pastry-less tart. It's easy to make: simply bake and top with pan-fried courgettes and creamy mascarpone. Serve with rocket.

Preheat the oven to 200°C/Fan 180°C/Gas 6 and grease a 25cm x 30cm rectangular baking tin (or 25cm round tin).

Heat the stock in a saucepan until boiling then pour in the polenta in a gradual, steady stream, stirring continuously until the mixture thickens. Season well, then leave to cool slightly. Press the polenta into the base and sides of the greased tin and bake for 10 minutes.

Meanwhile, heat a little olive oil in a frying pan and fry the courgettes until golden and softened. Add the garlic, cook for a minute, then remove from the heat and stir in the mascarpone and season.

Take the polenta out of the oven, top with the courgette and mascarpone mix and scatter over the grated Parmesan. Put it back in the oven for a further 15–20 minutes, until golden. Cut into squares and serve with rocket.

Per serving 363 kcals, **protein** 10.3g, **carbohydrate** 42.3g, **fat** 16.3g, **saturated fat** 10g, **fibre** 3g, **salt** 0.8g

Sweet potato and chilli tortilla

30 minutes | serves 2 | easy

1 sweet potato, peeled and
  cut into small cubes
1 tbsp oil
1 red chilli, finely chopped
  (deseeded if you like)
4 eggs
small handful of coriander,
  leaves chopped
75g feta, crumbled
green salad leaves, to serve
salt and freshly ground
  black pepper

This delicious sweet potato tortilla with a chilli kick and salty feta is meat-free and easy, making it a fantastic option for a quick meal. Serve with a green salad on the side.

Cook the sweet potato in a saucepan of simmering water for 4 minutes, then drain. Heat the oil in a frying pan and add the sweet potato and chilli. Fry for 2 minutes, then season. Beat the eggs in a bowl, season, then stir in the coriander.

Pour the eggs over the sweet potato and then crumble over the feta. Cook for 3 minutes, or until the base sets, then flash the top under a hot grill until it sets, but be careful with the handle when taking it out of the oven. Serve with a large, green salad.

Per serving 341 kcals, **protein** 19.4g, **carbohydrate** 18.2g, **fat** 20.6g, **saturated fat** 8.6g, **fibre** 2.8g, **salt** 1.8g

Halloumi, tomato and aubergine skewers

20 minutes, plus marinating | serves 2 | easy

1 garlic clove, crushed

½ bunch of parsley, leaves chopped

2 tbsp small capers, rinsed and roughly chopped

juice of ½ lemon

2 tbsp olive oil

6 cherry tomatoes

1 small aubergine, cut into 2cm cubes

100g low-fat halloumi, cut into 2cm cubes

crusty bread, to serve

handful of rocket leaves, to serve

salt and freshly ground black pepper

Given a boost with a simple marinade, these barbecued vegetarian halloumi skewers, piled onto crusty bread, will be a sure-fire hit.

Whisk the garlic in a bowl with the parsley, capers, lemon juice and oil, then season. Take out and reserve 2 tablespoons of the marinade, then toss the remaining marinade with the tomatoes, aubergine and halloumi. Season, then set aside to marinate for at least 20 minutes.

Thread the marinated tomatoes, aubergine and halloumi onto metal skewers. Heat a grill, griddle pan or barbecue to hot and sear the skewers for 2–3 minutes on each side, until the tomatoes just start to burst and the halloumi is golden.

Pile the skewers onto crusty bread and serve with rocket leaves and the remaining marinade poured over the top.

Per serving 276 kcals, **protein** 15.1g, **carbohydrate** 6.5g, **fat** 19.9g, **saturated fat** 6.7g, **fibre** 5.1g, **salt** 1.9

Warm roasted veg with spiced crushed chickpeas

30 minutes | serves 4 | easy

1 small butternut squash,
   peeled and chopped into
   bite-sized pieces
1 cauliflower head, broken
   into small florets
2 large parsnips, peeled
   and quartered
   lengthways
4 tbsp olive oil
1 tsp cumin seeds
1 tsp chilli flakes
2 x 400g cans of chickpeas,
   drained and rinsed
4 tbsp low-fat plain yoghurt
small bunch of flat-leaf
   parsley, leaves roughly
   chopped
small bunch of coriander,
   leaves roughly chopped
rice, couscous or
   flatbreads, to serve
salt and freshly ground
   black pepper

This dish is perfect as an accompaniment or a main dish. Serve with rice or couscous to keep with the Mediterranean feel.

Preheat the oven to 220°C/Fan 200°C/Gas 7. Toss the squash, cauliflower florets and parsnips with half the olive oil and season. Spread the vegetables out on a large baking tray. Bake for 25 minutes, until golden and completely cooked through.

Meanwhile, lightly toast the cumin seeds and chilli flakes. Add half of them to a frying pan with the chickpeas and heat through. Remove the pan from the heat, roughly crush the chickpea mixture using a potato masher and keep warm.

Mix the remaining cumin seeds and chilli flakes with the rest of the olive oil and some seasoning, to make a dressing. Stir the yoghurt and the herbs into the chickpeas and season. Serve the roasted veg with the crushed chickpeas and a drizzle of the chilli dressing. Serve with rice, couscous or flatbreads.

Per serving 408 kcals, **protein** 15.5g, **carbohydrate** 46.9g, **fat** 14.7g, **saturated fat** 2.3g, **fibre** 11.1g, **salt** 1.1g

Roasted squash and black bean tacos

30 minutes | serves 4 | easy

1 butternut squash, peeled, deseeded and cut into large dice
2 tbsp olive oil
1 tsp cumin seeds
½ tsp hot smoked paprika
400g can of black beans, drained and rinsed
8 corn tortillas
100g half-fat crème fraîche
grated zest and juice of 1 lime
sliced red onion and pickled jalepeño slices, to serve
salt and freshly ground black pepper

These vegetarian roasted squash and black bean tacos make for an easy veggie meal. Roasting squash brings out its natural sweetness, which balances nicely with the earthy beans.

Preheat the oven to 200°C/Fan 180°C/Gas 6. Toss the squash with the oil and spices, season, then spread out on a baking tray and roast for 15–20 minutes, or until tender. Tip the vegetables into a frying pan with the beans and heat through, stirring.

Warm the tortillas, then divide the squash mix between them. Mix the crème fraîche with the lime zest and juice, and season. Spoon a dollop onto each tortilla, then finish with onion and jalepeños.

Per serving 456 kcals, fat 10.6g, saturated fat 3.5g, carbohydrate 70.9g, fibre 11.5g, protein 13.3g, salt 0.9g

Feta and red pepper quinoa balls with lemon and dill aioli

30 minutes | serves 4 | easy

120g quinoa

olive oil, for frying

1 small red pepper, deseeded and finely chopped

2 tbsp pine nuts

grated zest and juice of 1 lemon

2 handfuls of dill, chopped

handful of mint, leaves chopped

100g feta, crumbled

1 egg

4 tbsp light mayonnaise

1 cucumber, halved, deseeded and sliced

4 large handfuls of salad leaves

salt and freshly ground black pepper

These quinoa balls are the veggie, healthy alternative to a meatball. Packed with feta, red pepper, mint and pine nuts, they are fresh-tasting and give a hint of the Mediterranean.

Preheat the oven to 220°C/ Fan 200°C/Gas 7 and line a baking sheet with baking parchment. Cook the quinoa according to the packet instructions, then drain well.

Heat a little oil in a frying pan and add the red pepper and pine nuts. Cook until the pepper has softened and the nuts are lightly golden.

Mix the cooked quinoa in a bowl with the lemon zest, 1 handful of the dill, the mint, fried pepper and nuts, the feta and egg. Season. Using your hands, carefully shape the mixture into balls the size of a walnut (you'll make about 30). Put them on the lined baking sheet and bake for 15 minutes, or until the tops are golden and they have firmed up.

To make the dressing, whisk the lemon juice with the mayonnaise and the remaining dill and season. Toss half the dressing with the cucumber.

To serve, divide the salad and cucumber between 4 plates. Add the quinoa balls (be gentle, as they are quite delicate) and drizzle over the remaining lemon and dill aioli.

Per serving 302 kcals, protein 12.2g, carbohydrate 21.4g, fat 18.4g, saturated fat 5.1g, fibre 2g, salt 1.4g

Cauliflower crust pizza

30 minutes | serves 2 | easy

½ cauliflower head, broken into florets
1 egg, lightly beaten
50g Parmesan cheese (or vegetarian alternative), grated
olive oil spray
½ garlic clove
pinch of red chilli flakes (optional)
250ml tomato passata
½ light mozzarella ball, thinly sliced
handful of basil leaves, finely chopped
handful of rocket or baby kale leaves, to serve
salt and freshly ground black pepper

This gluten-free, grain-free, low-carb pizza is made with cauliflower crumbs instead of flour. Top with your favourite pizza topping to make a fantastic healthy meal.

Preheat the oven to 200°C/Fan 180°C/Gas 6 and line a baking sheet with baking parchment.

Cook the cauliflower florets for 4 minutes in lightly salted boiling water, then drain well. Once cooled, pat with a kitchen towel to dry completely, and transfer to the bowl of a food processor. Blitz until it resembles couscous. Tip the cauliflower into a bowl, season and stir in the egg and Parmesan. Mix until it comes together. Spread onto the lined baking sheet, sprayed with oil and press into a round pizza-base shape using a spatula. Bake for 15–20 minutes until it is golden and feels firm.

Meanwhile, fry the garlic and chilli flakes, if using, with a few more sprays of the olive oil for 1 minute, then add the passata. Simmer and reduce until thick and spreadable. Add the basil and season. Spread the tomato sauce over the cauliflower 'pizza' crust then add the slices of mozzarella. Put the pizza back in the oven for 10 minutes to bake until the cheese has turned golden. Scatter with rocket or baby kale leaves to serve.

Per serving 357 kcals, **protein** 28.1g, **carbohydrate** 14.1g, **fat** 19.4g, **saturated fat** 10.4g, **fibre** 6.7g, **salt** 1g

Kale, lemon and pine nut linguine

20 minutes | serves 1 | easy

70g linguine
olive oil spray
1 shallot, sliced
1 garlic clove, crushed
grated zest and juice of
  ½ lemon
100g kale leaves, chopped,
  blanched and drained
1 tbsp toasted pine nuts
grated Parmesan cheese
  (or vegetarian
  alternative), to serve
salt and freshly ground
  black pepper

This recipe is perfect for one, but you can easily increase the quantities to serve more.

Cook the linguine according to the packet instructions, keeping back 2 tablespoons of the cooking water when draining.

Heat a frying pan, spray with oil and fry the shallot for 2 minutes, then add the garlic, lemon zest and kale and cook for a further minute. Add the drained linguine, the retained pasta water and the lemon juice, and toss with the kale. Season and scatter with pine nuts and a grating of Parmesan to serve.

Per serving 372 kcals, **protein** 15.1g, **carbohydrate** 47.8g, **fat** 13.2g, **saturated fat** 0.8g, **fibre** 1g, **salt** 0.2g

Chilli spinach noodles with sesame dressing

20 minutes | serves 2 | easy

2 medium egg noodle
nests
1 tbsp oil
1 red chilli, thinly sliced
(deseeded if you like)
1 garlic clove, crushed
200g spinach leaves,
roughly chopped

For the dressing
1 tbsp sesame seeds
½ tbsp soy sauce
1 tbsp Sake or mirin (if you
use mirin, omit the caster
sugar, below)
1 tsp caster sugar
½ tbsp water

This dish of chilli spinach noodles is quick and punchy. Try using rice or zero noodles if you want to reduce the calorie count even further.

To make the dressing, toast the sesame seeds in a dry frying pan until golden, then grind with a pestle and mortar. Stir in the remaining dressing ingredients, whisk and set aside.

Cook the noodles according to the packet instructions until just tender, then drain.

Heat the oil in a frying pan, add the chilli and garlic and cook for 2–3 minutes, stirring, then add the cooked noodles and toss to heat through. Stir in the spinach leaves and cook until wilted. Pile the noodles onto plates and spoon over the dressing.

Per serving 460 kcals, **protein** 16.7g, **carbohydrate** 78.9g, **fat** 6.1g, **saturated fat** 1.5g, **fibre** 7.2g, **salt** 2.3g

Spaghetti with balsamic roasted cherry tomatoes, capers and pine nuts

25 minutes | serves 4 | easy

400g cherry tomatoes
olive oil
3 tbsp balsamic vinegar
300g spaghetti
1 garlic clove, crushed
50g pine nuts
3 tbsp small capers, rinsed
salt and freshly ground
  black pepper

This quick recipe is perfect to put in the middle of the table and let your family or guests help themselves. Serve with a lightly dressed salad if you like.

Heat the oven to 180°C/Fan 160°C/Gas 4. Toss the tomatoes in a drizzle of olive oil, the vinegar and seasoning. Spread the tomatoes out on a baking tray and roast for 15 minutes. Cook the spaghetti according to the packet instructions.

Meanwhile, in a large frying pan, heat a little more oil and add the garlic, pine nuts and capers. Cook over a low heat for 2 minutes, or until the garlic and pine nuts begin to brown. Drain the spaghetti and add it to the pan along with the roasted tomatoes and their juices. Season, toss together and serve.

Per serving 405 kcals, **protein** 12.4g, **carbohydrate** 58g, **fat** 13g, **saturated fat** 1.3g, **fibre** 4g, **salt** 2g

Supergreen pasta with pecorino

20 minutes | serves 1 | easy

60g rigatoni or penne
50g asparagus spears,
   trimmed
1 tsp olive oil
2 spring onions, sliced
50ml white wine
50g spinach leaves
50g frozen peas, defrosted
1 tbsp low-fat soft cheese
1 tbsp chopped tarragon
   leaves
10g pecorino cheese
   (or vegetarian
   alternative), grated
salt and freshly ground
   black pepper

This supergreen pasta is packed with delicious veg and is full of flavour. It's perfect as a quick and easy meal after work, or you can easily bump up the quantities for a family meal.

Cook the pasta in lightly salted boiling water until al dente. Blanch the asparagus in lightly salted boiling water for 3 minutes until tender.

Heat the olive oil in a frying pan, add the spring onions and fry for 2 minutes. Add the wine and simmer for 3 minutes. Add the spinach and peas, and stir until the spinach has wilted. Season and stir in the soft cheese, the asparagus and the drained, cooked pasta. Stir through the tarragon, and sprinkle with the pecorino to serve.

Per serving 371 kcals, **protein** 18.6g, **carbohydrate** 40.7g, **fat** 9.9g, **saturated fat** 3.4g, **fibre** 6.3g, **salt** 0.6g

Spring onion tart with romesco sauce

30 minutes | serves 2 | easy

8–12 spring onions, trimmed and blanched for 2 minutes
olive oil
4 filo pastry sheets
100g fat-free Quark
1 tbsp grated Parmesan cheese (or vegetarian alternative)
½ garlic clove, crushed

For the romesco sauce
1 large roasted red pepper (from a jar)
½ red chilli, deseeded
1 plum tomato, chopped
½ garlic clove, chopped
2 tbsp blanched almonds, toasted
2 tbsp chopped flat-leaf parsley
½ tsp smoked paprika
1 tsp red wine vinegar
salt and freshly ground black pepper

This spring onion tart with romesco sauce looks stunning on the plate, but is actually very quick and simple to make. Romesco is an almond and red pepper sauce and it works really well with this tart, and you can also make extra to use as a topping for chicken or fish.

Heat the oven to 190°C/Fan 170°C/Gas 5 and line a baking sheet with baking parchment.

Blitz all the romesco sauce ingredients together in the bowl of a small food processor or in a small blender until combined, and season well. Add enough water to give it a drizzling consistency.

Heat a griddle pan to very hot, coat the spring onions with 1 teaspoon of olive oil, season and sear in the pan until charred and tender.

Lay the filo pastry sheets on top of each other, with a brush or spray of olive oil between each sheet. Put the filo sheets on the lined baking sheet, then scrunch up the sides to make a border.

Beat the Quark with the Parmesan and garlic until smooth, season, then spread over the filo tart base. Top with the charred spring onions. Cook in the oven for 15 minutes until the pastry is crisp and golden. Drizzle with romesco sauce and serve.

Per serving 449 kcals, **protein** 23g, **carbohydrate** 52.2g, **fat** 15.6g, **saturated fat** 2.8g, **fibre** 3.8g, **salt** 0.9g

Orecchiette with purple sprouting broccoli and wine sauce

25 minutes | serves 2 | easy

150g orecchiette

200g purple sprouting
broccoli spears, halved
lengthways if large

olive oil

1 red chilli, sliced
lengthways (deseeded
if you like)

2 garlic cloves, thinly sliced

175ml white wine

50g Parmesan cheese, half
finely grated and half
shaved

salt and freshly ground
black pepper

Orecchiette is a small, ear-shaped pasta that holds sauce very well, so it's perfect for this light dish.

Cook the pasta according to the packet instructions, adding the broccoli for the last 3 minutes of the cooking time.

While the pasta is cooking, heat a little oil in a frying pan, add the chilli and garlic and fry gently until lightly coloured and softened. Add the wine to the pan and simmer for 1 minute. Drain the pasta and broccoli. Tip them into the pan with the grated Parmesan, season, then toss everything together. Serve scattered with Parmesan shavings.

Per serving 467 kcals, **protein** 21.8g, **carbohydrate** 57.1g, **fat** 12.2g, **saturated fat** 5.5g, **fibre** 3.8g, **salt** 0.5g

Coconut and peanut aubergine curry

30 minutes | serves 4 | easy

1 tbsp oil, plus extra if needed

2 aubergines, cut into large chunks

2 onions, chopped

2 garlic cloves, crushed

5cm piece of fresh root ginger, finely grated

1 tsp cumin seeds

1 tsp coriander seeds, crushed

1 tsp ground turmeric

½ tsp chilli powder

400ml can half-fat coconut milk

1 tbsp tamarind paste

1 tbsp smooth or crunchy peanut butter

coriander leaves and bread or rice, to serve

This creamy coconut and peanut aubergine curry is so easy and full of flavour – it is a definite crowd pleaser, and a perfect comforting meal any time of year.

Heat the oil in a large frying pan. Add the aubergine in batches and fry until golden and soft. Add another tablespoon of oil if it starts to stick to the pan. Scoop the aubergine out of the pan once it is done and set aside.

Add the onion to the same pan and cook until soft and golden. Add the garlic and ginger and cook for 1 minute, then add the spices and cook for 2 minutes. Tip in the coconut milk, tamarind and peanut butter. Simmer gently until the peanut butter dissolves. Return the aubergine to the pan and simmer for 15 minutes. Sprinkle with coriander and serve with bread or rice.

Per serving 251 kcals, **protein** 5.5g, **carbohydrate** 17g, **fat** 15.5g, **saturated fat** 7.2g, **fibre** 10.6g, **salt** 0.1g

Jamaican sweet potato stew

30 minutes | serves 2 | easy

1 tbsp oil

4 spring onions, chopped
(including the green bits)

2 garlic cloves, crushed

¼–½ scotch bonnet chilli,
deseeded and finely
chopped

½ tsp ground allspice

½ tsp dried thyme

200ml coconut milk

1 large sweet potato,
peeled and cut into
bite-sized chunks

100g spinach leaves,
chopped

cooked rice, to serve

salt and freshly ground
black pepper

A quick curry recipe for weeknights. Vegetarian and filling, with big chunks of sweet potato and handfuls of spinach. Bulk it up with rice on the side.

Heat a little oil in a saucepan, add three-quarters of the spring onions and the garlic and fry until softened. Add the chilli, allspice, thyme and coconut milk. Simmer for 10 minutes. Add the sweet potato and cook for 8–10 minutes, or until tender.

Stir in the spinach and cook for a few more minutes. Season, then serve with rice, scattered with the remaining spring onions.

Per serving 356 kcals, **protein** 4.7g, **carbohydrate** 34.6g, **fat** 20.5g, **saturated fat** 15.6g, **fibre** 7.2g, **salt** 0.3g

Black bean chilli with guacamole and garlic ciabatta

30 minutes | serves 4 | easy

1 tbsp olive oil, plus extra
for drizzling
2 onions, chopped
3 garlic cloves, 2 crushed
and 1 left whole
2 green peppers, deseeded
and chopped
2 tbsp ground cumin
2 tsp chilli powder
2 x 400g cans of black
beans, drained and
rinsed
2 x 400g cans of chopped
tomatoes
200ml vegetable stock
2 large ripe avocados,
halved and stone
removed
grated zest and juice of
2 limes
4 spring onions, chopped
1 red chilli, finely chopped
(deseeded if you like)
8 slices of ciabatta, toasted
salt and freshly ground
black pepper

Full of flavour, you would be forgiven for thinking this recipe isn't healthy. It is perfect as a family winter warmer.

Heat the oil in a large frying pan. Add the onions, crushed garlic and green peppers, and fry for 10 minutes until softened. Add the spices and a pinch of salt and cook for a further minute. Tip in the beans, tomatoes and stock. Simmer for 15 minutes.

Meanwhile, scoop the flesh from the avocados into a bowl. Add the lime zest and juice, spring onions and chilli, season, and mix with a fork, to lightly mash the avocado.

Cut the remaining clove of garlic in half and use it to rub all over the toasted slices of ciabatta. Drizzle with olive oil, then pile the guacamole onto the toasts.

Serve the guacamole and garlic ciabatta alongside the chilli.

Per serving 489 kcals, **protein** 16.8g, **carbohydrate** 50.1g, **fat** 25.5g, **saturated fat** 4.9g, **fibre** 12.1g, **salt** 1.1g

Miso aubergine, green tea noodle and cucumber salad

30 minutes | serves 2 | easy

4 baby aubergines,
  quartered lengthways
1 tbsp brown miso paste
3 tbsp rice vinegar
1 tbsp runny honey
1 tsp grated root ginger
12cm piece of cucumber,
  quartered lengthways
  and cut into small chunks
100g green tea noodles or
  other noodles
1 tsp sesame oil
3 spring onions, sliced
handful of coriander,
  leaves roughly chopped
1 tbsp sesame seeds,
  toasted
salt and freshly ground
  black pepper

Light and fresh, miso and aubergine are a match made in heaven. This is perfect for lunch or a lighter supper.

Put a steamer over a pan of boiling water, tip in the aubergines, cover and steam for 8–10 minutes, or until they're really tender but still holding their shape. Mix the miso paste, 2 tablespoons of the rice vinegar, honey and ginger in a bowl. Gently toss with the steamed aubergines and set aside to marinate.

Mix the cucumber with the remaining tablespoon of rice vinegar, and stir occasionally while you cook the noodles in the pan of water you were steaming the aubergines over.

Drain the noodles well, and toss them with the sesame oil on a big platter to stop them sticking together. Drain the cucumber and tip it onto the noodles along with the aubergines and their marinade, the sliced spring onions, coriander and sesame seeds. Season then toss everything together and serve.

Per serving 210 kcals, **protein** 15g, **carbohydrate** 29.8g, **fat** 5.5g, **saturated fat** 0.9g, **fibre** 7.5g, **salt** 1.1g

No-fuss suppers

Jerk chicken with mango salsa

30 minutes | serves 2 | easy

¼ small white cabbage, shredded
juice of 1 lime
2 skinless chicken breasts
2 tbsp jerk paste
½ mango, peeled, stoned and diced
1 small shallot, finely chopped
1 tomato, deseeded and diced
¼ cucumber, deseeded and diced
¼ scotch bonnet chilli, deseeded and diced
2 tbsp chopped mint leaves
small bunch of coriander, leaves chopped
salt and freshly ground black pepper

Eating healthily doesn't mean you have to miss out on your favourite foods. This recipe for jerk chicken with mango salsa is packed full of flavour. It's so good, you'll forget you're being virtuous.

Heat the grill to high. Toss the cabbage with half the lime juice and season. Cover and leave at room temperature.

Brush the chicken breasts with the jerk paste and season well. Transfer the chicken to a lined baking tray and grill for 20 minutes, or until cooked through. Toss the diced mango with the shallot, tomato, cucumber and chilli. Season.

Stir the mint and coriander through the cabbage. Slice the chicken, then serve with the cabbage and mango salsa. Squeeze over the remaining lime juice.

Per serving 293 kcals, **protein** 34.4g, **carbohydrate** 20.2g, **fat** 6.9g, **saturated fat** 0.7g, **fibre** 5.8g, **salt** 0.8g

Quick-roast chicken with tomatoes, chickpeas and tarragon

30 minutes | serves 4 | easy

1 red onion, peeled and
  cut into thin wedges
250g cherry tomatoes
400g can chickpeas,
  drained and rinsed
4 skinless chicken breasts
1 tbsp oil
bunch of tarragon, leaves
  chopped
½ lemon, to serve
salt and freshly ground
  black pepper

This is the perfect mid-week supper - just tip the chicken breasts, cherry tomatoes and chickpeas into a tray and roast with tarragon. Dinner just doesn't get any easier than that!

Heat the oven to 200°C/Fan 180°C/Gas 6. Toss the onion, tomatoes, chickpeas and chicken breasts with the oil and season. Tip everything into a deep baking tray, and roast for 25–30 minutes, or until the chicken is cooked through, stirring through the tarragon for the last 10 minutes of the cooking time.

Remove the chicken breasts, slice thickly and place the slices on top of the veg. Squeeze over the juice from the half lemon to serve.

Per serving 265 kcals, **protein** 35.5g, **carbohydrate** 14.4g, **fat** 6.2g, **saturated fat** 1g, **fibre** 4.8g, **salt** 0.5g

Chicken burgers with pickled red cabbage

30 minutes | serves 4 | easy

½ small red cabbage,
very finely shredded
juice of 1 lime
3 tbsp rice vinegar
4 skinless chicken breasts,
chopped
1 tbsp chopped fresh root
ginger
small bunch of coriander,
leaves finely chopped
½ lemongrass stalk,
trimmed and finely
shredded
1 tsp sesame oil
2 tbsp sriracha chilli sauce,
plus extra to serve
4 tbsp panko breadcrumbs
1 tsp soy sauce
round lettuce leaves,
to serve
salt and freshly ground
black pepper

These Asian-inspired chicken burgers make a great healthy alternative to the usual beef. Pickled red cabbage adds an extra kick. Serve on round lettuce leaves instead of buns to make a carb-free meal.

Toss the shredded cabbage in a bowl with the lime juice and vinegar, and season. Put the cabbage to one side at room temperature until you're ready to serve. Preheat the oven to 220°C/Fan 200°C/Gas 7 and line a baking tray with baking parchment.

Place the chicken, ginger, coriander and lemongrass in the bowl of a food processor or in a blender and blitz briefly until combined. Add the sesame oil, sriracha, panko breadcrumbs and soy sauce and blitz again briefly, just enough to combine. Mould the mixture into 4 burgers, and place the burgers on the lined baking tray. Bake for 10–15 minutes on each side, until golden and cooked through. Serve on lettuce leaves, topped with the pickled cabbage and with extra sriracha on the side.

Per serving 231 kcals, **protein** 33.2g, **carbohydrate** 16.6g, **fat** 2.8g, **saturated fat** 0.5g, **fibre** 3.4g, **salt** 1.2g

Chicken in Parmesan crumbs with green beans

30 minutes | serves 2 | easy

2 skinless chicken breasts
2 tbsp grated Parmesan
  cheese
1 lemon, ½ zested and
  juiced, ½ cut into wedges
50g fresh breadcrumbs
1 egg, beaten
flour, for dusting
2 tsp olive oil
200g green beans,
  trimmed
1 garlic clove, crushed
bunch of parsley, leaves
  roughly chopped
salt and freshly ground
  black pepper

Similar to a schnitzel, this juicy chicken is baked rather than fried, meaning you can still have a crunchy coating on your chicken without the guilt.

Preheat the oven to 200°C/Fan 180°C/Gas 6. Put the chicken breasts between 2 sheets of baking parchment or cling film and, using a rolling pin or meat hammer, flatten them out to a thickness of approximately 1cm.

Mix the Parmesan, lemon zest and breadcrumbs in a wide, shallow bowl, and season well. Place the beaten egg in another wide, shallow bowl. One by one, dust the flattened chicken breasts with flour, dip them into the egg, then coat them in the breadcrumb mix.

Put the breaded chicken onto a baking tray, drizzle with 1 teaspoon of oil and bake for 20–25 minutes until the chicken is cooked through and the breadcrumbs are golden. Blanch the green beans in lightly salted boiling water for 3 minutes. Heat the remaining oil in a frying pan and fry the garlic gently for 1 minute, then add the cooked beans and lemon juice. Toss together well, and add the parsley, then serve with the chicken and lemon wedges.

Per serving 376 kcals, **protein** 44g, **carbohydrate** 22.1g, **fat** 11.3g, **saturated fat** 4.4g, **fibre** 5g, **salt** 1.2g

Rarebit pork with pea and watercress salad

20 minutes | serves 2 | easy

2 boneless pork loin steaks
   or chops, fat completely
   trimmed
75g Cheddar cheese,
   grated
½ tsp English mustard
dash of Worcestershire
   sauce
oil
salt and freshly ground
   black pepper

For the salad
4 spring onions, chopped
150g frozen peas,
   defrosted (pour over a
   kettleful of boiling water
   to do this quickly)
2 handfuls of watercress
1 tbsp olive oil
1 tbsp red wine vinegar

This recipe for rarebit pork with pea and watercress salad proves that you can still have your favourite foods while keeping healthy. Try making it with a thick slice of ciabatta rather than the pork if you want to enjoy a meat-free meal.

Put the chops between 2 sheets of baking parchment or cling film and, using a rolling pin or meat hammer, flatten them out to a thickness of about 1cm. To make the rarebit mix, combine the cheese, mustard and Worcestershire sauce and season well.

Rub the chops with oil and season, then cook them on a hot griddle or in a frying pan for 4 minutes on each side and cooked through.

Heat the grill to medium-high. When the chops are cooked, spread one side with the rarebit mix and put them under the grill until golden and bubbling.

For the salad, toss the spring onions, peas and watercress in the oil and vinegar and season. Serve with the pork.

Per serving 408 kcals, **protein** 40.5g, **carbohydrate** 7.8g, **fat** 22.6g, **saturated fat** 10.2g, **fibre** 6.1g, **salt** 1.1g

Pork chops with chimichurri and chipotle sweet potato mash

30 minutes | serves 2 | easy

400g sweet potatoes,
  peeled and chopped
1 tsp olive oil
2 lean pork chops,
  trimmed
1 tbsp chipotle paste
salt and freshly ground
  black pepper

For the chimichurri
½ small bunch of flat-leaf
  parsley
½ small bunch of oregano
½ garlic clove
½ tbsp red wine vinegar
2 tsp olive oil
salt and freshly ground
  black pepper

Pork chops make the best mid-week meal as they are so easy to prepare, but make a welcome change from your usual chicken dishes. Chimichurri is a green herb sauce from Argentina and can be used on any type of meat or fish.

Boil the sweet potatoes in lightly salted boiling water for 20 minutes, until very soft.

Meanwhile, to make the chimichurri, blitz the parsley, oregano, garlic, vinegar and oil in the bowl of a food processor or a small blender. Add a splash of water if needed, to combine, and season. Heat the grill to medium-high. Rub the oil into the pork chops and season.

Grill the chops for 3 minutes on each side, or until cooked through. Drain and mash the sweet potato, add the chipotle paste, mix well and season. Serve with the chops and the chimichurri spooned over the top.

Per serving 450 kcals, **protein** 38.3g, **carbohydrate** 41.9g, **fat** 12.2g, **saturated fat** 3.3g, **fibre** 7.4g, **salt** 0.5g

Teriyaki steak skewers with chopped green Asian salad

20 minutes, plus marinating | serves 2 | easy

1 tbsp soy sauce, plus extra
   for the salad
1 tbsp mirin
1 tsp runny honey
2 tbsp grated root ginger
400g lean diced sirloin
   steak, fat trimmed
1 large pak choi, shredded
½ cucumber, halved,
   deseeded and diced
1 spring onion, sliced
50g edamame, podded
1 tbsp sherry vinegar
1 tsp groundnut oil
steamed basmati rice,
   to serve
1 red chilli, deseeded and
   sliced, to serve
salt and freshly ground
   black pepper

These steak skewers are quick and juicy. Bump up the quantities if you are entertaining – it is sure to be a crowd pleaser.

Mix the soy sauce, mirin and honey in a bowl with half the grated ginger. Pour the marinade over the diced steak in a bowl and set aside to marinate for at least 1 hour.

Mix the pak choi, cucumber, spring onion and edamame in a bowl and toss with the sherry vinegar, groundnut oil, the remaining grated ginger and 1 teaspoon of soy sauce. Season.

Start your barbecue or heat a griddle pan to very hot, and thread the marinated steak onto small, soaked wooden skewers (about 4 pieces on each). Sear the steak for 2 minutes on each side, until charred and seared all over. Serve with the salad, steamed rice and chilli.

Per serving 372 kcals, **protein** 46.7g, **carbohydrate** 11.5g, **fat** 14.7g, **saturated fat** 5.5g, **fibre** 3.3g, **salt** 1.8g

Balsamic steaks with cherry vine tomatoes and sweet potato fries

30 minutes, plus marinating | serves 2 | easy

300g lean sirloin steak,
fat trimmed, cut into
2 pieces
3 tbsp balsamic vinegar
1 garlic clove, peeled and
halved
2 tsp picked thyme leaves
1 large or 2 small sweet
potatoes, peeled and cut
into skinny fries
1 tbsp oil, plus extra for
brushing
200g cherry vine tomatoes,
on the vine
salt and freshly ground
black pepper

A healthier alternative to your classic steak frites, but just as satisfying!

Place the steaks in a wide bowl. Mix the vinegar, garlic and thyme together, and pour the marinade over the steaks. Leave to marinate for at least 1 hour.

Heat the oven to 180°C/Fan 160°C/Gas 4 and line a baking tray with baking parchment. Toss the fries with the oil and season. Tip onto the lined baking tray and cook for 25 minutes, until crisp and golden.

Meanwhile, heat a griddle pan to very hot, brush the marinated steaks with 1 teaspoon of oil and cook for 2 minutes on each side (for medium steaks). Lift out and leave to rest.

Add the tomatoes to the griddle pan, sear for 4 minutes until almost bursting, pour in the leftover marinade and resting juices from the steak, reduce to a sauce, then pour over the steak and tomatoes. Serve with the sweet potato fries.

Per serving 379 kcals, **protein** 32.6g, **carbohydrate** 23.4g, **fat** 16.3g, **saturated fat** 4.6g, **fibre** 4.1g, **salt** 0.3g

Easy prawn and chorizo paella

30 minutes | serves 2 | easy

1 tbsp olive oil
1 onion, halved and sliced
6cm piece of chorizo,
   diced
150g bomba paella rice
600ml hot chicken stock
good pinch of saffron
   threads or ground
   turmeric
¼ tsp hot smoked paprika
150g raw prawns, peeled
75g roasted red peppers
   (from a jar), drained and
   chopped
big handful of parsley,
   leaves chopped
salt and freshly ground
   black pepper

Paella is one of those really comforting dishes that seems too complicated to make at home. Not true. This recipe for easy prawn and chorizo paella is ready to dish up in just 30 minutes, perfect for a quick meal. Plus, it comes in at under 500 calories.

Heat the oil in a deep frying pan, add the onion and cook for 5 minutes, or until soft. Add the chorizo and fry for a few minutes, then tip in the rice, most of the stock (leave a ladleful for adding later), saffron or turmeric, and paprika. Cover and cook for 12–15 minutes, until almost tender, then stir in the prawns, peppers and the remaining hot stock.

Cook for another 3–4 minutes, or until the prawns are pink and cooked through. Stir in the parsley, season and serve.

Per serving 464 kcals, **protein** 33.7g, **carbohydrate** 62.8g, **fat** 7.6g, **saturated fat** 2.9g, **fibre** 4.5g, **salt** 1.5g

Italian sausages with peppers, borlotti beans and rosemary

30 minutes | serves 2 | easy

olive oil

4 Italian or Toulouse
  sausages (or any herby,
  garlicky pork sausages),
  cut into chunks

1 onion, halved and sliced

1 tsp fennel seeds

½ tbsp chopped rosemary

2 roasted red peppers
  (from a jar), drained and
  sliced

400ml chicken stock

400g can borlotti beans,
  drained and rinsed

salt and freshly ground
  black pepper

One-pots are perfect for stress-free meals, and this recipe for Italian sausages with peppers, borlotti beans and rosemary is ready in just 30 minutes. Serve with crusty bread to soak up the juices.

Heat a little oil in a non-stick frying pan and brown the sausage chunks all over, then scoop out and set aside. Add the onion to the pan and cook until browned and soft. Add the fennel seeds and rosemary and cook for 1 minute, then add the red peppers and stock and bring to a simmer before returning the sausages to the pan.

Cook for 10 minutes then add the beans and cook for a further 10 minutes, until the sausages are cooked through. Season and serve with crusty bread.

Per serving 473 kcals, **protein** 38.1g, **carbohydrate** 26.3g, **fat** 21.5g, **saturated fat** 8.3g, **fibre** 11g, **salt** 2.2g

Louisiana red beans and rice

30 minutes | serves 4 | easy

oil
1 onion, diced
1 garlic clove, crushed
1 green pepper, deseeded
  and diced
2 celery sticks, trimmed
  and diced
200g cooked smoked
  sausage (Polish kabanos
  work well), cut into
  bite-sized chunks
½ tsp dried oregano
½ tsp dried thyme
1 tsp ground cumin
½ tsp hot smoked paprika
1 tbsp red wine vinegar
2 plum tomatoes, chopped
1 tbsp tomato purée
200ml chicken stock
400g can red kidney beans,
  drained and rinsed
cooked basmati rice,
  to serve
2 spring onions, chopped,
  to serve
salt and freshly ground
  black pepper

There are hundreds of different versions of this spicy Southern dish, but we think this is the best one out there.

Heat a little oil in a saucepan, add the onion and garlic and fry until soft. Stir in the green pepper and celery and cook for 3–4 minutes, then add the sausage and cook for 2 more minutes.

Add the dried herbs and spices and stir well, then add the red wine vinegar, tomatoes, purée and stock. Season. Simmer for 5 minutes, then tip in the beans and cook for a further 10–15 minutes. Serve with rice, sprinkling over the chopped spring onions to finish.

Per serving 249 kcals, **protein** 12.4g, **carbohydrate** 12.9g, **fat** 15.1g, **saturated fat** 4.9g, **fibre** 6.1g, **salt** 1.7g

Feta, chorizo and spring onion quesadillas

30 minutes | serves 2 | easy

2 plum tomatoes, diced
2 spring onions, chopped
   (including green bits)
small bunch of coriander,
   leaves chopped
4 pickled jalapeño slices
   (from a jar), finely
   chopped
juice of 1 lime
4 corn tortillas
100g feta, crumbled
100g chorizo, chopped
   into small pieces
salt and freshly ground
   black pepper

Quesadillas can be filled with all kinds of ingredients. This one is made with feta, chorizo and spring onions, but have a go with whatever filling ingredients you fancy. The chilli salsa on the side gives it a spicy kick.

Mix the tomatoes, spring onions and coriander in a bowl and season. Scoop out 3 tablespoons of the mixture and set to one side, then mix the rest with the jalapeños and lime juice to make a salsa.

To make the quesadillas, heat a large frying pan and put a tortilla on the bottom. Sprinkle over the feta, chorizo and the reserved tomato mixture, then top with another tortilla. Cook until the bottom is coloured and the cheese has started to melt (press down with a spatula to get the top tortilla to stick).

Flip the quesadilla over very carefully and brown the other side. Repeat with the remaining ingredients and tortillas. Cut into wedges and serve with the salsa.

Per serving 476 kcals, **protein** 23.7g, **carbohydrate** 44.2g, **fat** 22g, **saturated fat** 13.9g, **fibre** 3.3g, **salt** 3.1g

Roasted tomatoes and avocado on toast

30 minutes | serves 2 | easy

4 plum tomatoes, halved

4 thin slices of wholegrain or sourdough bread

1 small avocado, stoned, peeled and halved

½ lemon, juiced

pinch of cayenne pepper

handful of salad cress or baby rocket leaves, to serve

2 slices smoked salmon (optional)

This recipe requires few ingredients and little preparation so is perfect after a long day. Ripe tomatoes, avocado and salad leaves on toast make a great vegetarian combination, but you can it top with smoked salmon too if you like.

Heat the grill to medium-hot and grill the tomatoes for 20 minutes until soft. Toast the bread.

Using a fork, mash the avocado with lemon juice and cayenne pepper, then spread it over the toasted bread. Top with the tomatoes and some cress or baby rocket leaves and smoked salmon, if using.

Per serving 237 kcals, **protein** 5.4g, **carbohydrate** 27.8g, **fat** 10.6g, **saturated fat** 2.2g, **fibre** 4.2g, **salt** 0.6g

Runner beans with prawns and lemon

20 minutes | serves 2 | easy

300g runner beans, topped
    and tailed
oil
1 garlic clove, crushed
200g cooked peeled
    prawns
grated zest and juice of
    1 lemon
sesame oil
chilli oil
chilli flakes (optional)
2 tbsp flaked almonds,
    toasted
cooked rice, to serve
    (optional)
salt and freshly ground
    black pepper

Runner beans are at their best from June through to September, and come into their own in this summery recipe.

Cut the runner beans into fine long strips using a bean shredder or a sharp knife. Cook them for 2 minutes in lightly salted boiling water, then drain thoroughly.

Heat a little oil in a wok or large frying pan and add the garlic followed by the beans. Stir-fry over a high heat for 1 minute, then add the prawns and lemon zest.

Cook for another minute, then season with a splash of sesame oil, chilli oil and chilli flakes, if you like. Drizzle with lemon juice, sprinkle with flaked almonds, a little salt and freshly ground black pepper. Serve in bowls, with rice if you like.

Per serving 239 kcals, **protein** 20.6g, **carbohydrate** 4.4g, **fat** 14.8g, **saturated fat** 1.7g, **fibre** 3.8g, **salt** 2g

Prawn kedgeree

25 minutes | serves 2 | easy

150g basmati rice

oil

2 shallots, finely chopped

2 tsp madras curry powder

½ chicken stock cube

300ml water

150g cooked peeled
   prawns

2 hard-boiled eggs,
   quartered

knob of butter

2 tbsp chopped flat-leaf
   parsley

salt and freshly ground
   black pepper

Kedgeree is really quick and easy, but delivers on comfort. The spicy rice, juicy prawns and boiled eggs come together in a great balance of flavours.

Rinse the rice in cold water then let it soak in a fresh pan of cold water.

While the rice is soaking, heat a little oil in a frying pan, add the shallots and fry gently until they start to soften, then stir in the curry powder, crumble in the stock cube and cook for 1 minute. Drain the rice and add it to the pan with the water and bring it to a simmer. Cover and cook over a low heat for 10 minutes, or when the water has been absorbed.

Remove the lid and stir in the prawns, and sit the egg quarters on top, dot with a knob of butter and put the lid back on for a minute. Scatter over the parsley just before serving.

Per serving 433 kcals, **protein** 24.6g, **carbohydrate** 58.6g, **fat** 10.8g, **saturated fat** 3.2g, **fibre** 1.5g, **salt** 2.1g

Spicy prawn linguine

30 minutes | serves 2 | easy

1 tsp olive oil
2 shallots, diced
1cm piece of fresh root
   ginger, peeled and grated
1 garlic clove, crushed
large pinch red chilli flakes
400g can of chopped
   tomatoes
150g linguine
½ bunch of flat-leaf parsley,
   leaves chopped
150g raw peeled prawns
rocket leaves, to serve
salt and freshly ground
   black pepper

This spicy prawn linguine has a chilli kick to trick your taste buds so you won't need heaps of pasta on your plate.

Heat the oil in a large frying pan, add the shallots and fry for 2 minutes then add the ginger, garlic and chilli flakes. Fry for a further 2 minutes. Add the chopped tomatoes and simmer for 20 minutes.

Meanwhile, cook the linguine in lightly salted boiling water until just tender, then drain. Stir the parsley and prawns into the tomato sauce, season well and cook until the prawns turn pink. Add the cooked linguine, toss and serve with a rocket salad.

Per serving 326 kcals, **protein** 24.1g, **carbohydrate** 46.6g, **fat** 4.1g, **saturated fat** 0.3g, **fibre** 2.8g, **salt** 0.6g

Cajun blackened fish with trinity slaw

30 minutes | serves 2 | easy

2 skinless white fish fillets
3–4 tsp Cajun spice mix, or
   a mix of equal quantities
   of smoked paprika, garlic
   salt, dried thyme and
   ground black pepper
butter, for frying
salt and freshly ground
   black pepper

For the trinity slaw
½ small white cabbage,
   cored and shredded
½ sliced green pepper,
   deseeded and thinly
   sliced
½ small onion, sliced
2 celery sticks, trimmed
   and finely sliced
2 tsp cider vinegar or white
   wine vinegar
1 tbsp mayonnaise
pinch of salt

This is a classic Cajun dish. The trinity in this is the onion, celery and green pepper – a combination that forms the basis of so much Cajun cooking. It's easy to bump up the quantities for this recipe and use the full amount of your ingredients for the slaw.

Toss all the slaw ingredients together in a bowl with a generous pinch of salt. (It might not look like a lot of mayo, but keep tossing until everything is coated.)

Sprinkle the fish on both sides with the Cajun spice mix, then melt some butter in a non-stick frying pan and fry the fish on both sides until cooked through and dark golden brown.

Pile the slaw on 2 plates and sit the fish on top to serve.

Per serving 273 kcals, **protein** 28g, **carbohydrate** 8.4g, **fat** 13.1g, **saturated fat** 3.9g, **fibre** 4.6g, **salt** 0.8g

Hot-smoked salmon cakes with caper dressing

30 minutes | serves 3 | easy

3 medium floury potatoes,
　peeled and chopped
grated zest and juice of
　½ lemon, plus wedges
　to serve
2 spring onions, sliced
2 tbsp chopped dill, plus
　extra to serve
2 skinless hot smoked
　salmon fillets, flaked
olive oil spray
2 tbsp plain flour
4 tbsp low-fat yoghurt
2 tbsp small capers, rinsed
　and chopped
handful of salad leaves,
　to serve
salt and freshly ground
　black pepper

Salmon fishcakes are a classic and here they are as a guilt-free meal. The caper dressing is quite punchy, so you only need a drizzle.

Cook the potatoes in lightly salted boiling water for 10–15 minutes, until tender. Drain the potatoes and leave them to steam in the colander for 2 minutes, uncovered, to dry out. Mash, and stir in the lemon zest, spring onions, half the chopped dill and the flaked hot smoked salmon. Season well and shape into 6 patties.

Heat a frying pan and spray with olive oil. Dust the patties in the flour then fry them for 5 minutes on each side until golden and hot throughout.

Mix the yoghurt, capers, remaining chopped dill and lemon juice and season. Serve with the fishcakes, more dill, a few lemon wedges and a salad.

Per serving 293 kcals, **protein** 22.5g, **carbohydrate** 40.3g, **fat** 3.9g, **saturated fat** 0.7g, **fibre** 3.7g, **salt** 3.7g

Roast cod with olives, capers and tomatoes

20 minutes | serves 2 | easy

200g green beans,
trimmed
2 tbsp olive oil
2 pieces of skinless
sustainable cod or
haddock loin
½ tsp chopped rosemary
8 green fruity olives, pitted
and quartered
2 tsp small capers, rinsed
and drained
2 tomatoes, diced
juice of ½ lemon
salt and freshly ground
black pepper

This Mediterranean-inspired recipe for roast cod with olives, capers and tomatoes is super-healthy.

Cook the green beans in lightly salted boiling water until just tender. Drain, and keep warm in the pan.

Heat the oil in a non-stick frying pan. Season the fish, then cook for 3–4 minutes on each side, until cooked through. Transfer the fish to a plate and keep warm under foil.

Add the remaining ingredients, except the lemon juice, to the frying pan, season and cook for 1 minute. Add the lemon juice and bubble for another minute. Sit the fish on the beans and spoon over the sauce.

Per serving 275 kcals, **protein** 29.9g, **carbohydrate** 4.9g, **fat** 14.1g, **saturated fat** 2.1g, **fibre** 4.6g, **salt** 1.6g

Thai coconut fish parcels

25 minutes | serves 2 | easy

200g tenderstem broccoli

2 large sustainable white
fish fillets (about 150g
each)

small chunk of fresh root
ginger, peeled and
shredded

1 lemongrass stalk, woody
outer layers removed and
inner core finely chopped

1 red chilli, finely chopped
(deseeded if you like)

3 spring onions, sliced

200ml reduced-fat coconut
milk

2 tsp fish sauce

The Asian-inspired flavours of these Thai coconut fish parcels ensure that you can eat inspiring food even when you're short of time or watching your weight.

Preheat the oven to 200°C/Fan 180°C/Gas 6. Blanch the broccoli in lightly salted boiling water until just tender then drain.

Tear 2 squares of baking parchment and 2 squares of foil. Sit the paper on top of the foil. Put the blanched broccoli in the centre, sit the fish on top, and scatter over the ginger, lemongrass, chilli and spring onions.

Mix the coconut milk and fish sauce together and spoon the mixture over each piece of fish. Scrunch up the paper into a parcel to seal and cook for 20 minutes, or until the fish is cooked through.

Per serving 244 kcals, **protein** 33.7g, **carbohydrate** 5g, **fat** 9.1g, **saturated fat** 6.6g, **fibre** 4g, **salt** 1.3g

Cod in parsley and lemon butter sauce

30 minutes | serves 2 | easy

300g new potatoes,
  scrubbed
1 small shallot, finely
  chopped
1 tbsp white wine vinegar
100ml chicken stock
50g butter, diced
½ lemon
1 tbsp chopped flat-leaf
  parsley leaves
2 thick pieces of boneless,
  skinless cod or haddock
olive oil
2 handfuls of watercress,
  chopped
salt and freshly ground
  black pepper

This recipe makes the most of classic flavour combinations. Leave out the new potatoes and serve with lots of green veggies if you want to go carb-free.

Cook the potatoes in lightly salted boiling water until tender. While the potatoes are cooking, put the shallot and vinegar in a small saucepan and simmer until the vinegar has evaporated. Add the chicken stock and bring to a simmer. Gradually whisk in the butter, then add a squeeze of lemon. Mix in the parsley.

Heat the grill to high. Rub the fish with oil and season, then grill for 5 minutes until it is just cooked through. Drain the potatoes, then gently crush them with some seasoning. Mix in the watercress.

Divide the potato between 2 plates. Sit the fish on top and spoon over the sauce.

Per serving 497 kcals, **protein** 41.7g, **carbohydrate** 26.2g, **fat** 24.3g, **saturated fat** 13.7g, **fibre** 3.4g, **salt** 1g

Grilled mackerel with chickpea salad

30 minutes | serves 2 | easy

1 tbsp olive oil, plus extra
  for brushing
1 onion, sliced
1 tbsp garam masala
400g can chickpeas,
  drained and rinsed
2 x 100g mackerel fillets
½ lemon
handful of rocket leaves,
  to serve
salt and freshly ground
  black pepper

Fresh grilled mackerel makes the perfect fish supper when served on top of this easy chickpea and rocket salad. Add a squeeze of lemon to really bring it to life.

Heat the oil in a frying pan, add the onion and fry for 20 minutes, until golden and caramelised. Stir in the garam masala and cook for 1 minute, then add the chickpeas with a splash of water, stir to coat the chickpeas, and season. Cook for another 5 minutes, until most of the water has evaporated.

Heat the grill to high. Brush the mackerel fillets with a little oil, season and grill for 5 minutes, until cooked through.

Squeeze the lemon over the chickpeas and serve with the mackerel and a few rocket leaves.

Per serving 486 kcals, **protein** 29.7g, **carbohydrate** 27.1g, **fat** 27g, **saturated fat** 4.4g, **fibre** 8g, **salt** 0.9g

Roast trout fillets with herb couscous

20 minutes | serves 2 | easy

200ml hot vegetable stock
75g couscous
2 skinless trout fillets,
    pin-boned
1 tsp olive oil
1 lemon, ½ thinly sliced
    and ½ juiced
bunch of dill, chopped,
    plus a few sprigs
4 tbsp pomegranate seeds
2 tomatoes, diced
½ bunch of mint, leaves
    chopped
½ bunch of parsley, leaves
    chopped
salt and freshly ground
    black pepper

This dish is packed full of flavour. The pomegranate seeds provide a great, juicy crunch and the herby couscous gives it a fresh, Mediterranean feel.

Preheat the oven to 220°C/Fan 200°C/Gas 7. Pour the hot stock over the couscous in a heatproof bowl, cover with cling film and set aside. Rub the trout fillets with the oil and season.

Lay half the lemon slices and a few dill sprigs on a baking tray covered with foil and put the trout on top. Roast for 6–8 minutes, until cooked through.

Fluff up the couscous with a fork and tip in the pomegranate seeds, tomatoes, mint, parsley, chopped dill and lemon juice. Divide the couscous between 2 plates and top each with a roasted trout fillet.

Per serving 349 kcals, **protein** 30.9g, **carbohydrate** 26.7g, **fat** 12.4g, **saturated fat** 2.8g, **fibre** 3.5g, **salt** 0.3g

Blackened cod with radish slaw

20 minutes | serves 1 | easy

8 radishes, thinly sliced
¼ small red cabbage, shredded
½ small red onion, thinly sliced
1 celery stick, trimmed and thinly sliced
small bunch of coriander, leaves chopped
1 jalapeño chilli, deseeded and sliced (or sliced from a jar)
juice of 1 lime
2 tsp olive oil
1 tsp smoked paprika,
1 tsp ground cumin
1 tsp dried oregano
½ tsp garlic or celery salt
200g piece skinless of sustainable cod fillet
salt and freshly ground black pepper

This cod is super-easy, ready in just 20 minutes, and comes in at under 300 calories, making it perfect as a meal for one. Bump up the ingredients to serve for family or friends.

Mix the radishes, cabbage, red onion, celery, most of the coriander and jalapeño slices in a large bowl. Whisk the lime juice with half of the oil and some seasoning. Tip the mixture into the slaw and toss.

Mix the spices and garlic or celery salt together and rub the mix over the fish, coating it all over. Heat the remaining oil in a frying pan until very hot, and sear the cod on each side for 2 minutes until the spices darken, and the fish is cooked through. Serve with the remaining coriander and the radish slaw.

Per serving 292 kcals, **protein** 41.4g, **carbohydrate** 13.5g, **fat** 6.4g, **saturated fat** 0.8g, **fibre** 7.8g, **salt** 2.9g

Guilt-free takeaways

Spiced grilled paneer with roti and a cabbage salad

30 minutes | serves 3 | easy

1 tsp groundnut oil

small piece of fresh root ginger, peeled and finely grated

200g pack paneer, cut into bite-sized cubes

12 baby plum tomatoes

½ tsp ground cumin

½ tsp ground coriander

½ tsp mild chilli powder

½ tsp ground turmeric

3 roti or chapatis, warmed to serve

natural yoghurt and lime pickle, to serve

salt and freshly ground black pepper

For the cabbage salad

¼ small white cabbage, finely shredded

½ red onion, finely sliced

juice of 1 lemon

½ tsp cumin seeds, toasted

pinch of salt

Paneer is an unsalted white cheese that's very common in vegetarian Indian dishes. Here it is spiced and served with warm bread and a simple cabbage salad.

To make the salad, toss everything together with a good pinch of salt. Leave to sit while you cook the paneer.

Mix the oil with the ginger in a bowl, add the paneer and tomatoes, season and toss. Sprinkle over the dry spices, toss again, then leave for 10 minutes.

Heat the grill to high. Push the paneer and tomatoes onto metal skewers, season with salt and freshly ground black pepper, then put them on a baking sheet and grill for 7–8 minutes, turning the skewers until the paneer is golden and the tomatoes are soft. Serve with the salad, roti or chapatis, yoghurt and pickle.

Per serving 174 kcals, **protein** 16.7g, **carbohydrate** 9.2g, **fat** 7.1g, **saturated fat** 3.7g, **fibre** 3.5g, **salt** 0.1g

Coconut chickpea curry

30 minutes | serves 4 | easy

1 onion, diced
1 garlic clove
thumb-sized piece of fresh
   root ginger, peeled
1 red chilli, sliced
   (deseeded if you like)
oil
½ tsp ground turmeric
1 tsp garam masala
1 tsp ground cumin
1 tsp ground coriander
400g butternut squash,
   peeled, deseeded and
   cut into 1cm cubes
400g can chickpeas,
   drained and rinsed
160ml half-fat coconut
   milk
250ml water
50g mangetout
100g spinach
1 lime, cut into wedges,
   to serve
steamed rice, to serve
salt and freshly ground
   black pepper

The best quick vegetarian curry. Full of good-for-you ingredients, this will tempt any veg-phobic family members to dig in. Serve with rice on the side.

Place the onion, garlic, ginger and chilli in the bowl of a small food processor or a blender and pulse to form a paste. Heat 1 teaspoon of oil in a large frying pan and fry the paste for 2 minutes, then add the spices, toast for 1 minute, stir in the squash and fry for a further 5 minutes.

Add the chickpeas, coconut milk, water and season, then cover and simmer for 20 minutes, until the squash softens. Add the mangetout and spinach, and stir for 2 minutes until the spinach wilts. Serve with lime wedges and rice.

Per serving 191 kcals, **protein** 7.5g, **carbohydrate** 23.6g, **fat** 5.6g, **saturated fat** 2.5g, **fibre** 8g, **salt** 0.5g

Chicken saag

30 minutes | serves 4 | easy

2 red chillies, deseeded
2 garlic cloves
4cm piece of fresh root
   ginger, peeled
1 onion, chopped
1 tsp oil
1 tsp ground cumin
1 tsp ground coriander
1 tsp garam masala
½ tsp ground turmeric
4 cloves
4 skinless chicken breasts,
   cut into bite-sized pieces
150g red split lentils
400g can chopped
   tomatoes
260g spinach, chopped
4 small rotis or naan,
   warmed, to serve
salt and freshly ground
   black pepper

This chicken saag recipe is easy to make and needs few ingredients. It also comes in at under 500 calories, so it's perfect if you are on a calorie-restricted diet, but equally as delicious even if you're not!

Put the chillies, garlic, ginger and onion in the bowl of a small food processor or a blender and pulse to form a paste. Heat the oil in a large frying pan and fry the paste for 2 minutes, stirring, until fragrant. Add the spices and cook for a further minute.

Add the chicken pieces and coat them in the spices. Cook for 5 minutes then add the lentils and chopped tomatoes along with 1½ cans of water. Simmer for 20–25 minutes, season, then tip in the spinach and stir until wilted. Serve with rotis.

Per serving 330 kcals, **protein** 42.8g, **carbohydrate**, 27.9g, **fat** 3.8g, **saturated fat** 0.6g, **fibre** 6.2g, **salt** 0.6g

Prawn masala with spinach roti

30 minutes | serves 2 | easy

1 onion, chopped

1 garlic clove

5cm piece of fresh root
   ginger, grated

small bunch of coriander

1 tsp oil

400g can of chopped
   tomatoes

150g raw king prawns,
   peeled

juice of 1 lemon

salt and freshly ground
   black pepper

For the masala

1 dried chilli, or pinch
   of red chilli flakes

1 tsp ground cumin

1 tsp crushed black
   peppercorns

½ tsp ground turmeric

1 tsp ground coriander

For the spinach roti

150g wholemeal bread
   flour, plus extra for
   dusting

1 tsp olive oil

100g spinach, blanched,
   drained and finely
   chopped

75ml cold water

This simple prawn masala proves that you can eat healthily without having to miss out on your favourite takeaway foods.

To make the roti, mix the flour, oil and spinach with a pinch of salt and the water. Knead on a lightly floured work surface until you have a smooth dough. Leave to rest for 10 minutes.

Make the masala by mixing the spices together.

Put the onion, garlic, ginger and most of the coriander in the bowl of a small food processor or a blender and pulse until they form a paste. Heat the oil in a frying pan and fry the paste until fragrant, then add the masala spice mix. Fry for a further minute then add the tomatoes. Bring to a simmer and cook for 10 minutes until thickened.

Divide the rested roti dough into 2 pieces, and roll each piece on a lightly floured surface into a thin bread. Dry-fry the bread in a frying pan for 3 minutes on each side, until cooked and starting to puff up. Keep warm while you finish the curry.

Stir the prawns into the curry and cook until pink, then season with lemon juice, salt and freshly ground black pepper, and scatter over the remaining coriander.

Per serving 440 kcals, **protein** 29.2g, **carbohydrate** 59.5g, **fat** 6.4g, **saturated fat** 0.8g, **fibre** 13.8g, **salt** 1g

Salmon tikka with radish raita

20 minutes | serves 1 | easy

oil spray
4 tbsp fat-free yoghurt
1 tsp grated fresh root
  ginger
½ garlic clove, crushed
1 tsp tandoori masala mix
½ tsp ground cumin
1 skinless salmon fillet
  (about 150g)
lemon wedges, to serve
salt and freshly ground
  black pepper

For the raita
¼ cucumber, halved,
  deseeded and grated
1 tbsp chopped mint
  leaves
6 radishes, thinly sliced

Spice up your mid-week dinner with this recipe for salmon tikka with radish raita. It's super-easy and ready in just 20 minutes – bump up the quantities for a meal for two or a family meal.

Heat the grill to high and lightly spray a baking tray with oil. Put the grated cucumber in a sieve and squeeze out most of the water. Leave to drain.

Mix 1 tablespoon of the yoghurt with the ginger, garlic and spices, then season. Rub the mixture over the salmon fillet, put the fillet onto the oiled baking tray and grill for 4–6 minutes, or until cooked through and the edges begin to char.

Mix the raita ingredients together with the remaining 3 tablespoons of yoghurt and season. Serve with the grilled salmon, and lemon wedges to squeeze over the top.

Per serving 401 kcals, **protein** 40.5, **carbohydrate** 16g, **fat** 19.1g, **saturated fat** 3.2g, **fibre** 1.4g, **salt** 0.7g

Tamarind prawn curry

20 minutes | serves 2 | easy

1 tsp coriander seeds, toasted
1 tsp cumin seeds, toasted
1 tbsp oil
1 small onion, halved and thinly sliced
pinch of salt
thumb-sized piece of fresh root ginger, peeled and grated
1 garlic clove, crushed
½ tsp ground turmeric
200ml coconut milk
2 tbsp tamarind paste
1 green chilli, finely sliced (deseeded if you like)
180g raw peeled prawns
coriander leaves, to serve
rice, to serve
chapatis, warmed, to serve

Here's a prawn curry that's ready for the table in under 30 minutes, and you're even making your own spice paste! Serve with rice and chapatis.

Grind the toasted seeds with a pestle and mortar. Heat the oil in a frying pan and cook the onion with a pinch of salt until soft and golden. Add the ginger, garlic, turmeric and ground seeds then fry for 1 minute.

Pour in the coconut milk, add the tamarind and chilli and simmer for 5 minutes.

Tip in the prawns, cover and cook for 3–4 minutes, or until they turn pink. Sprinkle with coriander and serve with rice and chapatis.

Per serving 361 kcals, **protein** 18.6g, **carbohydrate** 15.3g, **fat** 24.8g, **saturated fat** 15.9g, **fibre** 1.2g, **salt** 0.7g

Thai red fish curry with broccoli

20 minutes | serves 4 | easy

1 tbsp oil
2 shallots, diced
1 lemongrass stalk, bashed
2–3 tbsp red Thai curry paste
400g can of reduced-fat coconut milk
4 sustainable skinless white fish fillets (about 100g each)
230g tenderstem broccoli
lime wedges, to serve
salt and freshly ground black pepper

This dish gives just enough curry taste to keep you satisfied but not overwhelm the fish or your taste buds. Serve with steamed rice, if you like.

Heat the oil in a frying pan and fry the shallots for 1 minute, then add the bashed lemongrass and the curry paste. Fry for a further minute, stirring. Add the coconut milk and simmer for 10 minutes, until the sauce thickens.

Add the fish, cover and cook for 3–4 minutes, until the fish is cooked through. Blanch the broccoli in a separate pan of lightly salted boiling water for 4 minutes, then divide it between 4 plates. Add the fish, season, then pour over the sauce and serve with the lime wedges.

Per serving 235 kcals, **protein** 28g, **carbohydrate** 3.3g, **fat** 11.8g, **saturated fat** 6.1g, **fibre** 1.9g, **salt** 0.6g

Asian pork meatball noodles

30 minutes | serves 2 | easy

2 egg noodle nests

300g lean minced pork

small piece of fresh root
  ginger, peeled and grated

½ small garlic clove,
  crushed

pinch of red chilli flakes
  (optional)

sesame oil

½ red pepper, deseeded
  and sliced

100ml chicken stock

soy sauce

4 spring onions, sliced

salt and freshly ground
  black pepper

**These Asian-flavoured meatballs are easy to make and when tossed
with egg noodles, make a filling but not overly sweet fakeaway.**

Cook the noodles according to the packet instructions until just tender,
then rinse under cold running water and drain well.

Put the minced pork in a bowl with the ginger, garlic, chilli flakes, if using,
and a couple of drops of sesame oil. Season, then mix well and roll into
about 12 small balls.

Heat a little more oil in a frying pan and fry the meatballs all over until
golden and cooked through. Scoop them out and set them aside, then add
the pepper to the pan and stir-fry it for a few minutes.

Return the meatballs to the pan with the stock and a splash of soy sauce,
and bring to a simmer. Add the noodles and toss to heat through.
Serve topped with the spring onions.

Per serving 439 kcals, **protein** 36g, **carbohydrate** 32.9g, **fat** 17.5g, **saturated fat** 6.1g, **fibre** 2.8g, **salt** 1.3g

Vietnamese bun cha

30 minutes, plus marinating | serves 4 | easy

4 spring onions, chopped

walnut-sized piece of fresh
root ginger, peeled and
roughly chopped

2 garlic cloves, roughly
chopped

1 pork fillet (about 350g),
trimmed and cut into
long, thin strips

2 tbsp fish sauce

1 tbsp soy sauce

1 tsp sesame oil

For the dipping sauce

2 tbsp golden caster sugar

2 tbsp rice vinegar

2 tbsp fish sauce

2 tbsp water

juice of 1 lime

1 red bird's eye chilli,
chopped (deseeded if
you like)

To serve

cooked vermicelli rice
noodles (served cold)

Little Gem lettuce leaves

sprigs of coriander

sprigs of mint

blanched bean sprouts

'Bun cha' is a popular salad in Vietnam. It's very easy to prepare, as the sizzling pork is served with a make-ahead salad of cold noodles, herbs and bean sprouts and a punchy dipping sauce.

Put the spring onions, ginger and garlic in the bowl of a small food processor or a blender and pulse to form a paste. Mix the paste with the pork strips in a bowl, and add the fish sauce, soy sauce and sesame oil. Toss everything together, cover and chill for a couple of hours or overnight.

Thread the pork onto 12 wooden or metal skewers (soak the skewers in water first if using wooden ones), concertinaing it as you go, then cook the pork on a griddle pan or barbecue until caramelised and cooked through.

Mix the dipping sauce ingredients together.

Put a pile of each accompaniment onto 4 plates, then add the pork skewers and a bowl of dipping sauce to each.

Per serving 302 kcals, **protein** 48.3g, **carbohydrate** 12.9g, **fat** 6.3g, **saturated fat** 2.2g, **fibre** 0.3g, **salt** 4g

Vietnamese caramelised pork

30 minutes | serves 2 | easy

2 tbsp soft dark brown
    sugar
2 tbsp fish sauce
1 tbsp soy sauce
1 shallot, finely chopped
1 garlic clove, crushed
2 pork chops, fat trimmed
150g cooked rice noodles
½ small cucumber, cut into
    batons
1 tbsp rice wine vinegar
1 red chilli, thinly sliced,
    to serve
handful of mint leaves,
    to serve

**This Vietnamese-inspired caramel pork recipe is quick and easy,
and looks so good it feels like a treat.**

Put the sugar, fish sauce, soy sauce, shallot and garlic in a large dish with
a splash of water. Mix well, then add the chops and leave to marinate for
15 minutes, turning them now and again. Heat the grill to high.

Put the marinated chops on a baking tray and grill, brushing them with
the marinade frequently, until they are cooked through, glazed and sticky.

Toss the rice noodles and cucumber with the vinegar and divide the
noodle mixture between 2 plates. Slice the pork and sit it on top. Scatter
over the chilli and mint leaves to serve.

Per serving 493 kcals, **protein** 53.1g, **carbohydrate** 42.5g, **fat** 11.7g, **saturated fat** 3.6g, **fibre** 2.6g, **salt** 4.7g

Broccoli and pork soba noodles

30 minutes, plus marinating | serves 4 | easy

4 tbsp oyster sauce

2 tbsp soy sauce

1 tbsp runny honey

thumb-sized piece of fresh root ginger, peeled and grated

2 garlic cloves, crushed

1 pork tenderloin (about 350g), trimmed

2 tsp groundnut oil

1 red chilli, deseeded and diced

2 spring onions, sliced

1 head of broccoli, broken into florets and blanched for 2 minutes

150g cooked soba noodles

Soba noodles are made from buckwheat flour and make the perfect base for any healthy stir-fry.

Mix 3 tablespoons of the oyster sauce, half of the soy sauce, the honey and half the ginger and garlic in a bowl. Pour the mixture over the pork and leave to marinate for at least 1 hour.

Preheat the oven to 200°C Gas/Fan 180°C/Gas 6. Heat half the oil in a frying pan and fry the marinated pork for 10 minutes, turning it over halfway through cooking, until well browned on all sides. Transfer the pork to a baking tray and roast for 10–15 minutes, until cooked through. Remove and set aside to rest.

Meanwhile, heat the remaining oil in a frying pan and stir-fry the chilli with the remaining ginger and garlic for 2 minutes, then add the spring onions and the blanched broccoli and cook for a few minutes more. Stir in the remaining oyster sauce and soy sauce and stir-fry for 3 minutes. Add the noodles to warm them through for a minute, divide them between 4 bowls, slice the pork and place it on top.

Per serving 390 kcals, **protein** 37.6g, **carbohydrate** 36.5g, **fat** 10.4g, **saturated fat** 2.7g, **fibre** 4.9g, **salt** 4.4g

Yaki udon noodles

20 minutes | serves 2 | easy

1 tbsp oil

4 spring onions, shredded

1 red pepper, deseeded and cut into strips

200g broccoli, cut into very small florets and blanched

½ tbsp grated fresh root ginger

1 garlic clove, crushed

1 x 150g pack of udon noodles, rinsed to separate

For the sauce

2 tbsp soy sauce

2 tbsp mirin

1 tbsp Worcestershire sauce

1 tsp tomato ketchup

¼ tsp caster sugar

Stir-fries are the best quick meal. Get all your ingredients ready before you start, then the cooking takes just minutes. Healthy and vegetarian, this speedy stir-fry is made with broccoli, peppers, ginger, garlic and udon noodles, but you can add chicken if you like.

Heat the oil in a large frying pan or wok. Add the spring onions and red pepper and stir-fry for a couple of minutes, then add the blanched broccoli, ginger and garlic and cook for a further minute.

Mix the sauce ingredients in a bowl and add the sauce to the pan, along with the noodles. Toss everything together until heated through.

Per serving 374 kcals, **protein** 12.4g, **carbohydrate** 57.8g, **fat** 9.2g, **saturated fat** 1g, **fibre** 8.8g, **salt** 3.5g

Ponzu-glazed tuna with apple cucumber salad

20 minutes | serves 6 | easy

6 tbsp Japanese soy sauce

6 tbsp lime juice

6 tbsp mirin

3 tbsp golden caster sugar

6 tuna steaks (about 125g each)

2 tsp sesame oil

2 tbsp sesame seeds (black or white)

steamed rice, to serve (optional)

salt and freshly ground black pepper

For the salsa

1 Granny Smith apple, cored and julienned

1 tbsp lime juice

1 firm but ripe mango, flesh julienned

2 celery sticks, trimmed and julienned

½ cucumber, deseeded and julienned

small bunch of chives, snipped

Ponzu is a citrus-based Japanese sauce. Using it to glaze tuna makes for a really delicious meal that looks great, feeds a crowd and is ready in just 20 minutes.

Make a ponzu glaze by mixing the soy sauce, lime juice, mirin and sugar in a small saucepan. Heat for about 5 minutes, or until the sugar has dissolved and the mixture is syrupy, then remove from the heat. Spoon a little glaze over the tuna steaks and rub it into the flesh, along with the sesame oil. Sprinkle with the sesame seeds and season.

Heat a barbecue, grill or griddle pan to very hot. Mix the apple with a little lime juice and toss with the mango, celery, cucumber and chives. Grill the tuna steaks for 1–2 minutes on each side, keeping the centre quite rare. Serve with rice, the salsa and the remaining ponzu glaze to pour over everything.

Per serving 458 kcals, **protein** 33.1g, **carbohydrate** 53.5g, **fat** 11.6g, **saturated fat** 2.4g, **fibre** 3.5g, **salt** 5.6g

Index

Photography credits

SOUPS AND SALADS

Iced green gazpacho with summer salsa *Ant Duncan*
Spring greens, lemon and tortellini broth *Sam Stowell*
Carrot soup with wild garlic pesto *Philip Webb*
White bean and spring green one-pot *Lara Holmes*
Broccoli soup with Stilton toasts *Stuart Ovenden*
Prawn and mushroom miso soup *Stuart Ovenden*
Hot-and-sour fish soup *Ant Duncan*
Pan-fried halibut with summer vegetable broth *Ant Duncan*
Smoked pollock and parsnip chowder *Adrian Lawrence*
Morrocan smoky squash stew *Adrian Lawrence*
Roots and ham hock soup *Sam Stowell*
Za'atar roasted aubergine with puy lentil salad *Lara Holmes*
Warm broad bean, pea, baby leek and prosciutto salad with eggs *Lara Holmes*
Pear, pecan and dolcelatte salad *Claire Winfield*
Veggie chopped cobb salad *David Munns*
Watercress, spinach and green apple salad with buttermilk dressing *Philip Webb*
Winter greens and grains salad *Claire Winfield*
Three bean and feta salad with coriander and jalapeño dressing *Ant Duncan*
Grilled aubergine sabich salad *Ant Duncan*
Butterhead salad with home-made salad cream *Sam Stowell*
Spiced yoghurt chicken and grain salad *Stuart Ovenden*
Thai chicken noodle salad *Stuart Ovenden*
Steak and winter greens *Ant Duncan*
Green goddess salad *Adrian Lawrence*
Smoked salmon and quails egg Caesar salad *Sam Stowell*
Smoked trout and cannnelini bean salad *Stuart Ovenden*
Smoked trout and asparagus Niçoise *David Munns*
Sea bass Thai noodle salad *Philip Webb*
Smoked mackerel and roasted beetroot salad *Stuart Ovenden*
Crab and fennel salad with mandarin dressing *Stuart Ovenden*

VERY SPEEDY MEALS

Egg white omelette with kale and sweet potato *Stuart Ovenden*
Avocado and smoked salmon toasts *Stuart Ovenden*
Sourdough with spinach, egg and mustard *Adrian Lawrence*
Super store-cupboard salad *Lara Holmes*
Courgetti with pesto and balsamic tomatoes *Stuart Ovenden*
Halloumi with caper, lemon and chilli dressing *Ant Duncan*
Broccoli, chilli and lemon wholewheat pasta *Adrian Lawrence*
15-minute Szechuan pork *Stuart Ovenden*
Pork saltimbocca *Ant Duncan*
10-minute steak tacos *Stuart Ovenden*
Chargrilled chilli prawns with cucumber salad *Gareth Morgans*
Thai smoked trout salad *Adrian Lawrence*
Griddled tuna with pineapple salsa *Lara Holmes*

MEAT-FREE MEALS

Leek, mushroom and spinach soufflé omelette *Maja Smend*
Broccoli and roasted red pepper frittata *Stuart Ovenden*
Spinach and feta chickpea pancakes *Stuart Ovenden*
Kale and sweet potato hash *Sam Stowell*
Creamy courgette and polenta tart *Adrian Lawrence*
Sweet potato and chilli tortilla *Ant Duncan*
Halloumi, tomato and aubergine skewers *Ant Duncan*

Warm roasted veg with spiced crushed chickpeas *Maja Smend*
Roasted squash and black bean tacos *Sam Stowell*
Feta and pepper quinoa balls with lemon and dill aioli *David Munns*
Cauliflower crust pizza *Stuart Ovenden*
Kale, lemon and pine nut linguine *Lara Holmes*
Chilli spinach noodles with sesame dressing *Sam Stowell*
Spaghetti with balsamic roasted cherry tomatoes, capers and pine nuts *Lara Holmes*
Supergreen pasta with pecorino *Stuart Ovenden*
Spring onion tart with romesco sauce *Stuart Ovenden*
Orecchiette with purple-sprouting broccoli and wine sauce *Maja Smend*
Coconut and peanut aubergine curry *Lara Holmes*
Jamaican sweet potato stew *Sam Stowell*
Black bean chilli with guacamole and garlic ciabatta *Dan Jones*
Miso aubergine, green tea noodle and cucumber salad *Stuart Ovenden*

NO-FUSS SUPPERS

Jerk chicken with mango salsa *Lara Holmes*
Quick-roast chicken with tomatoes, chickpeas and tarragon *Stuart Ovenden*
Chicken burgers with pickled red cabbage *Stuart Ovenden*
Chicken in parmesan crumbs with green beans *Lara Holmes*
Rarebit pork with pea and watercress salad *Sam Stowell*
Pork chops with chimichurri and chipotle sweet potato mash *Lara Holmes*
Teriyaki steak skewers with chopped green Asian salad *Stuart Ovenden*
Balsamic steaks with cherry vine *Lara Holmes*
Easy prawn and chorizo paella *Stuart Ovenden*
Italian sausages with peppers, borlotti beans and rosemary *Lara Holmes*
Louisiana red beans and rice *Sam Stowell*
Feta, chorizo and spring onion quesadillas *Adrian Lawrence*
Roasted tomatoes with avocado on toast *Stuart Ovenden*
Runner beans with prawns and lemon *Philip Webb*
Prawn kedgeree *Ant Duncan*
Spicy prawn linguine *Stuart Ovenden*
Cajun blackened fish with trinity slaw *Adrian Lawrence*
Hot-smoked salmon cakes with caper dressing *Stuart Ovenden*
Roast cod with olives, capers and tomatoes *Gareth Morgans*
Thai coconut fish parcels *Sam Stowell*
Cod in parsley and lemon butter sauce *Sam Stowell*
Grilled mackerel with chickpea salad *Stuart Ovenden*
Roast trout fillets with herb couscous *Stuart Ovenden*
Blackened cod with radish slaw *Stuart Ovenden*

GUILT-FREE TAKEAWAYS

Spiced grilled paneer with roti and salad *Sam Stowell*
Coconut chickpea curry *Adrian Lawrence*
Chicken saag *Lara Holmes*
Prawn masala *Stuart Ovenden*
Salmon tikka with radish raita *Lara Holmes*
Tamarind prawn curry *Adrian Lawrence*
Thai red fish curry with broccoli *Lara Holmes*
Asian pork meatball noodles *Sam Stowell*
Vietnamese bun cha *Sam Stowell*
Vietnamese caramelised pork *Sam Stowell*
Broccoli and pork soba noodles *Gareth Morgans*
Yaki udon noodles *Sam Stowell*
Ponzu-glazed tuna with apple cucumber salad *Ant Duncan*